God's Voice Within

Other Books by Mark E. Thibodeaux, SJ

Armchair Mystic:
Easing into Contemplative Prayer

God, I Have Issues:
Fifty Ways to Pray No Matter How You Feel

God's Voice Within

The Ignatian Way to Discover God's Will

Mark E. Thibodeaux, SJ

LOYOLAPRESS.
A JESUIT MINISTRY

Chicago

LOYOLA PRESS.
A JESUIT MINISTRY

3441 N. Ashland Avenue
Chicago, Illinois 60657
(800) 621-1008
www.loyolapress.com

Scripture quotations contained herein are from the New Revised Standard Version Bible: Catholic Edition, copyright © 1993 and 1989 by the Division of Christian Education of the National Council of the Churches of Christ in the U.S.A. Used by permission. All rights reserved.

Quotes from *The Spiritual Exercises* are from *The Spiritual Exercises of St. Ignatius*, translated by Louis J. Puhl (Chicago: Loyola Press, 1951). Used by permission.

Unless otherwise indicated, quotes from the autobiography of St. Ignatius of Loyola are from *A Pilgrim's Journey: The Autobiography of Ignatius of Loyola*, translated by Joseph N. Tylenda, SJ (San Francisco: Ignatius Press, 2001). Used by permission.

Prayer Exercise D: Praying with Gratitude, which appears on page 144–145, first appeared in *God, I Have Issues: 50 Ways to Pray No Matter How You Feel*, by Mark E. Thibodeaux (Cincinnati, OH: St. Anthony Messenger Press, 2005), p. 84. Used by permission.

Library of Congress Cataloging-in-Publication Data
Thibodeaux, Mark E.
 God's voice within : the Ignatian way to discover God's will / Mark Thibodeaux.
      p. cm.
  ISBN-13: 978-0-8294-2861-2
  ISBN-10: 0-8294-2861-5
  1.   Discernment of spirits. 2.   God (Christianity)--Will. 3.   Decision making--Religious aspects--Catholic Church. 4.   Ignatius, of Loyola, Saint, 1491-1556. Exercitia spiritualia.   I. Title.
  BV5083.T45 2010
  248.3--dc22

                                                    2010022856

Printed in the United States of America
        14 15 Bang 10 9 8 7 6 5

This book is dedicated to the mentors and friends of my own support network. You know who you are. I hope you know how grateful I am to you.

Contents

Acknowledgments

This book is filled with stories of myself and of other people. When appropriate, I have acquired permissions and have changed names, places, and situations. Please note, too, that since the purpose of all these stories is to illustrate the relevant point rather than to write an accurate nonfiction story, some of the stories are entirely made up, others are entirely true and accurate, and still others are some mixture of fiction and nonfiction. I told the story that would best illustrate the point. I thank all the people who have given me permission to use one snippet or another from their lives. I am deeply grateful.

The eight people who were my biggest help and inspiration during the writing and editing of the manuscript were Lee Ann Badum; Jerry Fagin, SJ; Christopher Harris; William F. Huete, SJ; James Martin, SJ; my parents, Carroll and Shirley Thibodeaux; and my Loyola Press editor, Vinita Wright. I am deeply grateful for their generosity to me. I am also grateful for the many friends and communities who offered their love, support, wisdom, and counsel. Among them are Paul Deutsch, SJ; Michael Dooley, SJ; Dan White, SJ; Sister Kathleen Farrelly, O. Carm.; Mr. and Mrs. Robin and Easton Hebert; the novices of Grand Coteau from 2007 to 2010 (especially Caleb Bernacchio, Marc Fryer, Jonathan Harmon, and Peter Gadalla); the Catholic community at the University of Texas Pan American; as well as the Jesuit communities of St. Charles College of Grand Coteau, Louisiana; Loyola University of New Orleans; Strake Jesuit of Houston; and Spring Hill College of Mobile, Alabama. Finally, thank you to my loving family: Steve, Annette, Cameron, Demi, Greg, Nancy, Ashley, Dillon, Stuart, Stacey, Abbie, Michael, Eric, Sandy, Marty, and Coy.

Writing this third book of mine was a delightful and challenging experience. The subject matter demanded that I work even harder on it than on my previous books. The experience, I believe, has made me a better writer and a better discerner. I am deeply grateful to God for calling me to such a project. I pray that this book will give God ever-greater glory—ever greater praise, reverence, and service.

Foreword:
Decision Making by Heart

James Martin, SJ

*W*hat should I do?

How many times have you asked yourself that question today? How about during this week? this month? this year? over the course of your life?

In a sense, it is *the* question we ask ourselves, again and again. It applies to major decisions: *Where should I go to college? What should I study? What career path should I take? What job should I take?* It applies to decisions about our personal, and most intimate, relationships: *How should I treat my parents? How should I respond to a friend in crisis? What should I do about the problems in my marriage?* And it applies to more common, but no less stressful, situations: *When should I confront my annoying boss? How should I approach that soured relationship in my family? What should I do about my crazy neighbor?*

But decision making is not only about "shoulds." It also concerns our heartfelt wants, our deepest desires, our holy longings. If we are self-reflective people, we ask ourselves other questions as well: *Who do I want to become? What do I most want to do with my life? Who is God calling me to be?*

Most of us would agree that these are essential questions. But if we're honest, most of us would also admit that these questions can be difficult, stress inducing, even terrifying. Sometimes we get paralyzed by such questions, and fearing the need to make important decisions, we postpone them, avoid answering them fully, or simply ignore them. Decisions can overwhelm us.

If only, we think, *there were an easy-to-use guide to help us make these big, overwhelming, life-changing decisions—and the small ones, too.*

Fortunately, there is.

St. Ignatius of Loyola was a sixteenth-century soldier-turned-mystic who founded the Catholic religious order known as the Jesuits. As you'll soon read, Ignatius was a keen student of human nature, a beloved spiritual master, and a superb decision maker. Through his own experiences (both in his daily life and in his prayer), he came to understand an important truth: God desires for us to make good decisions and will help us do so. All we need to do, besides having a good intention, is not only rely on our (literally) God-given reason but also pay attention to the movements of our heart, which was also given to us by God. St. Ignatius poured his considerable insights on decision into his great spiritual classic, *The Spiritual Exercises.*

The sum total of these insights on making a good decision is known as Ignatian discernment. Ignatius's way includes well-ordered series of practices, techniques, and skills that understand that good decision making is a combination of faith and reason. You trust your heart, as one Jesuit once said, but use your head, too.

In the past, however, Ignatian discernment was too often presented as overly complex, full of complicated strategies and arcane techniques, cloaked in high-flown language, almost as if you needed to have a PhD and a flowchart just to *begin* to understand it. And that's too bad, because Ignatian discernment isn't that complicated. An authentic spirituality is a simple spirituality. After all, when asked about the kingdom of God, Jesus gave his disciples stories about weeds and wheat, not a six-hundred-page theological treatise! His were profound, mysterious answers but were still able to be understood by his listeners.

That's why this book is so welcome. As you will soon discover, Mark Thibodeaux, SJ, is one of the friendliest, most welcoming, and most accessible guides to decision making you could imagine. Using abundant examples from his own life (and his own considerable experience helping others in spiritual direction) as well as from the life of Ignatius, he opens up the riches of Ignatian discernment to help you to decide what you should (and shouldn't) do. Or where you want (and don't want) to go.

Mark's facility with Ignatian spirituality is evident to anyone who has ever met him. One of the liveliest and most lighthearted Jesuits I know (and a good friend), Mark is the perfect example of how holiness leads to joy. His full life—as a teacher, a spiritual director, a novice master, and a priest—shows that by making good decisions, we can bring ourselves closer to God. And moving closer to God means moving closer to a life of peace—and joy. It's almost impossible to feel downhearted or downcast when you're with Mark, and some of the times in my life when I've laughed the loudest have been with him.

But Mark would no doubt be embarrassed to have the focus placed on him. He would probably move our attention to St. Ignatius, who would shift the focus where it belongs: God. Ultimately, this book is centered on God: how God can help us make important decisions, how God can move our hearts to "discern" well, how God can be found in all the different "spirits" that move our lives. How God's voice can be found within.

God wants us to make life-giving decisions, and so God will help us to that end. That's one of the underlying themes of this useful, accessible, and entirely enjoyable new book.

So the next time you say to yourself, with some distress, *What should I do?* don't despair. Take a deep breath, pick up this book, use your head, and trust your heart.

James Martin, SJ, is a Jesuit priest, culture editor of *America* magazine, and author of the best-selling books *The Jesuit Guide to (Almost) Everything* and *My Life with the Saints*.

Why Read This Book?

You are probably reading this book because you have recognized a need in your own life for wiser discernment. We tend to think of discernment as decision making, but discernment goes much deeper and broader than simply making choices. True discernment teaches us to make honest assessments of our situations and problems. True discernment teaches us to be self-aware; otherwise, we will get in the way of our own wise choice making. True discernment is not only a matter of reason but also a matter of spirituality. It involves every aspect of our person, from emotion to analysis, from desire to resistance, from personal will to personal prayer.

Discernment would be simple if we could identify the five, or twelve, or twenty-five fail-proof steps to making good choices. But choices are not the result of mere rational exercise; choices come out of who we are as well as out of what we think. That is why discernment is not a system but a process, and it's a process we must learn, and apply, and then learn some more.

The Ordinary, Daily Decisions

You make hundreds of decisions on a daily basis—ordinary choices about ordinary things.

- **How you will fill up your day:** Should I work hard today or take it easy? In my work, how do I distinguish between what's most important from what's irrelevant?
- **How you might serve Christ:** Should I spend the afternoon visiting my elderly aunt, writing my congressperson, or working on this important project? Should I again wash my family

member's dirty dishes or push him to do it himself? Should I write a check to this charity or save my money until I'm financially secure? Should I spend more time in prayer or get more work done today?

- **How you might take good care of yourself today:** Should I take the morning off or get right to work? Should I allow myself dessert, or should I abstain? Should I see a doctor about this pain, or should I toughen up and see if it goes away on its own? Should I go for a run this evening or spend more time with the people I love? Should I watch the game on TV this afternoon or play with my kids in the backyard?

- **How you will relate to other people:** Should I confront my friend about this problem, or should I let it go? Should I check up on my son in college or wait for him to 'check in' himself? Should I defend myself when criticized today, or should I listen quietly and consider what is said? Should I apologize for my behavior or stand up for it?

- **What sort of attitude you should have:** At work, should I be ambitious and assertive or quiet and humble? Should I challenge the boss or suck it up? Should I push those under my authority to work harder, or should I ease up on them? At home, should I stay angry at this family member, or should I let it go? Do I allow myself to be sad about this loss, or should I dry my tears and get on with it?

You are well aware of the consequences of these seemingly insignificant choices. If you say the wrong thing at the wrong moment to the wrong person—which you often do—you might well set off all-out war. You know that if you ease up on your work, those who demand more of you will be angry or disappointed. You know that your elderly aunt will not be around forever and that your children will grow up too fast. You know that you're good to no one when you let yourself burn out and never allow yourself to relax. You know that God wants you to be good to yourself, to treat yourself occasionally, but you are also aware of your own temptations to overindulge.

More crucial than those consequences are the extent to which these seemingly small and insignificant daily choices *define who you are as a person*. Are you lazy, hardworking, or a workaholic? Are you a pushover, lovingly firm, or downright bossy? Are you passive, prudent, or overaggressive? Are you self-loathing, realistic about yourself, or self-serving? Are you kind, cold, or a flatterer? You know well that all of these important questions about your character—about who you are as a person—are defined at least as much by the small daily decisions as by the big momentous ones.

Also, you are aware that the accumulation of these small decisions, added to the totality of others' decisions, may eventually yield disastrous or glorious results. We pollute the earth one bag of trash or one corporate-waste policy at a time. A Hitler rises to power, not all at once and by force, but over time and with the support of ordinary citizens.

African-Americans in the 1960s did not suddenly gain full rights through one momentous decision but rather through a serious of small decisions made by ordinary people—people such as Rosa Parks, who, one ordinary day, decided to have a seat in the front of the bus, and by ordinary white people who gradually chose to resist prejudice within themselves when the likes of a Rosa Parks sat beside them on the bus.

When an earthquake devastated the nation of Haiti in 2010, a person could contribute to relief efforts simply by cell-phone texting the word *Haiti* to a certain number. This method of donation was promoted everywhere on TV, radio, and the Internet. Ordinary people, while surfing the Web, flipping channels on TV, or sitting at a stoplight, each pledged a mere ten dollars to relief efforts. In a matter of days, millions of dollars were raised.

You know that ordinary people's choices—of which leaders to support and oppose, of how to feel about the person sitting on the bus beside them, of how to spend ten measly dollars—literally changed the course of world history. As a Christian, you feel compelled to make the right choices no matter how small those choices might seem on any given day. You are confronted with scores of such choices *every single day* of your life, and yet you have spent little time considering *how* to go about making these decisions. You have no *method* for making such decisions. Instead, you simply take a stab in the dark—or worse, you let life dictate to you how you will act. You have a sense that you should be proactive in the way you decide to behave in one moment or another, but you have no idea of how to go about consciously, prayerfully deciding such things.

The Big Decisions

You look back on your life and see that there were momentous choices that propelled your life in irrevocable directions:

- The choice to break up with or marry someone
- The choice to stay in your hometown or move to a distant city
- The choice to pursue this career or that one
- The choice to have this many children or that many
- The choice to attend this church or that one
- The choice to have sex or to abstain
- The choice to stop drinking or smoking or to have "just one more"
- The choice to enter the seminary or to pursue family life

You know that in some of these momentous choices, you actually discerned well and acted assertively on that good discernment. But you are also painfully aware of the bad choices you made—the bad marriage, the that voice. They will not follow a stranger, because they know that the stranger's voice is not the voice of their good shepherd. The great Bible commentator William Barclay gives a vivid description of this image. In first-century Palestine, each shepherd had a unique call that his own sheep recognized immediately. Sometimes at night, several flocks were herded together into a cave for protection. In the morning, how would the sheep be sorted? The shepherds would stand a distance from one another and begin calling their sheep. By hearing the various voices, the sheep could immediately detect the voice of their shepherd and follow him (William Barclay, *Bible Commentary*, vol. 2, p. 57).

In any given situation, whether in an ordinary day or in a day of momentous decision, there are many voices in your head and heart proposing to you a variety of actions, reactions, or nonactions. The Ignatian method of discernment teaches you how to fine-tune your spiritual senses so that you can more readily detect and move toward the voice of the Good Shepherd, distinguishing that voice from all the others.

What You Can Expect

This book is divided into three major parts. Part 1 (chapters 2–3) introduces the reader to St. Ignatius of Loyola and tells how he came to develop his method of discernment. It then introduces the two types of voices, the true spirit and the false spirit, and the two states of being, consolation and desolation, which accompany these voices. The reader learns to detect consolation and desolation by learning the characteristics of these two opposing states of being.

Once you are able to detect the spirits within you, what are you to do with them from day to day? What do you do when you find yourself in desolation, that is, under the influence of the false spirit? What do you do when you are in consolation, that is, under the influence of the true spirit?

Part 2 (chapters 4–5) presents Ignatius's teaching on how to respond to the state of being in which you find yourself on any given day.

How can you use this Ignatian intuition to make a big decision? Part 3 teaches the methods of determining God's will through recognizing the source of the voices pulling you toward or away from any given option. It presents the disposition you need to work toward before beginning to discern (chapter 6), the path a typical discernment usually takes (chapter 7), and the work you must do after coming to a decision (chapter 8).

At the end of the book you'll find an index of the figures, stories, and prayer exercises used throughout the book, a glossary of Ignatian terms, a listing of Scripture passages that address the topic of discernment, an annotated bibliography of books on Ignatian discernment, and the primary text of Ignatius's Rules for Discernment of Spirits.

> In returning and rest you shall be saved; in quietness and in trust shall be your strength. . . . [The Lord] will surely be gracious to you at the sound of your cry; when he hears it, he will answer you. . . . Your Teacher will not hide himself any more, but your eyes shall see your Teacher. And when you turn to the right or when you turn to the left, your ears shall hear a word behind you, saying, "This is the way; walk in it." (Isaiah 30:15, 19–21)

PART 1

The True and False Spirits

In addition to being universally regarded as one of the great mystics of the church, St. Ignatius of Loyola is sometimes called "the world's first psychologist." Long before the world had an understanding of the psyche and a vocabulary to describe the interior life, Ignatius seemed to have a grasp of what goes on deep within our thoughts and emotions. He did not have a psychological vocabulary to work with; instead, he used the language of spirituality and mysticism. I suspect that even if he'd possessed the vocabulary of psychology, he would have chosen to describe our inner movements in terms of good and evil. Why? Because he was convinced that, psychology notwithstanding, all our thoughts, feelings, and actions are moving us either closer to God or further away from God. The church believes this still.

But how did "Ignatian spirituality" get started? What was Ignatius of Loyola's first inkling that we humans experience subtle movements in our souls?

It all started with a cannonball.

Iñigo de Loyola was born into a noble family of the Basque region of Spain around the year 1491. His upbringing was full of the stuff of medieval court life: gallant battles, alluring women, shining armor, all-important honor, sword fights, card games, and lots of alcohol—not a great start for a saint! Iñigo was known for his tremendous passion and zeal, but he squandered it on selfish pursuits and petty, doomed battles.

In 1521, he found himself rousing his fellow soldiers to keep fighting in defense of the fortress of Pamplona, despite their imminent defeat. When a cannonball hit Iñigo in the leg, the Spaniards immediately gave up the fight. The conquering army allowed Iñigo to be taken back to his castle in Loyola to recover. This fiery soldier was to spend many weeks alone in bed with nothing to do.

In his boredom, he asked for novels about romance and noble warfare, but there were only two books in the house—one on the lives of the saints and another on the life of Christ. During those long lonely hours in bed, Ignatius found himself deep in the revelry of daydreams. Sometimes, he would dream of himself as a heroic nobleman: fighting important battles for a feudal lord, winning the hand of a lady of high nobility, holding prestigious positions in a mighty kingdom. Other times, his religious books would lead him to imagine himself as a new St. Francis or St. Dominic: fighting battles against the prince of evil; pledging undying loyalty to the heavenly Lord; asking Mary, the mother of Christ, to be his queen.

Then one day he had an epiphany: he noticed an important distinction between the way he felt after his chivalric dreams and the way he felt after dreaming of religious life. Referring to himself in the third person, Ignatius describes this extraordinary moment of insight:

> There was this difference, however. When he thought of worldly matters, he found much delight; but after growing weary and dismissing them, he found that he was dry and unhappy. But when he thought of . . . imitating the saints in all the austerities they practiced, he not only found consolation in these thoughts, but even after they had left him he remained happy and joyful. He did not consider nor did he stop to examine this difference until one day his eyes were

partially opened, and he began to wonder at this difference and to reflect upon it. From experience he knew that some thoughts left him sad while others made him happy, and little by little he came to perceive the different spirits that were moving him; one coming from the devil, the other coming from God.

—*A Pilgrim's Journey: The Autobiography of*
Ignatius of Loyola, 48

This recognition of "the difference between the two spirits that moved him" became the foundation of Ignatius's lifelong exploration of how a person discerns God's will. He came to believe that God, in infinite love and compassion for us, is at all times stirring our hearts with desires to do great deeds of life and love while another spirit leads us to lower dreams and moves us to act against the life-giving inspirations of God. Ignatius discovered that if a person could simply discern between these two spirits—the one pulling toward life and the other pulling away from life—then that person would know God's will. He noticed that the pull toward the good has distinctive characteristics that reveal God, its ultimate source. The pull away from God, too, has distinctive characteristics. The more a person can detect these characteristics, the easier it is to recognize and follow the true spirit toward life in God.

The Two Spirits

The next two chapters will explore the characteristics of these two spirits: the **false spirit**, often referred to by Ignatius as "the evil spirit" or "the enemy of our human nature," and the **true spirit**, often referred to as "the good spirit."

It is important to understand that Ignatius's idea of the false spirit seemed to be broader than what is commonly referred to as the devil, although the devil would surely be included in the definition. Jesuit Father William Huete puts it this way: The false spirit equals the devil *plus* the trauma of tragic circumstances such as cancer or hurricanes, *plus* destructive experiences and behaviors, *plus* psychological baggage, *plus* emotional weaknesses, and so on. The false spirit is anything that draws me away from God and from God's loving plan for the world.

Likewise, when referring to the true spirit, Ignatius was speaking not only of the Holy Spirit but also of anything else that would draw me closer to God. The true spirit equals the Holy Spirit *plus* good in the world, *plus* happy life circumstances such as good health or sunny weather, *plus* life-affirming experiences and behaviors, *plus* psychological well-being and strength.

The false spirit: The "inner pull" away from God's plan and away from faith, hope, and love. The false spirit is also referred to as "the evil spirit" or "the enemy of our human nature."	**The true spirit:** The "inner pull" toward God's plan and toward faith, hope, and love. It is also referred to as "the good spirit."

When I snap at my father, is it because the "devil" moves me to do so or because of some childhood psychological wound or because I didn't get a good night's rest last night? My answer to this question is *yes*! All these factors combine to pull me away from God. This influence, we call the false spirit or the evil spirit.

Using Ignatius's understanding of the interior life, we say that when a person is under the influence of the false spirit, he or she is in a state of desolation. We will explore this in detail in chapter 2.

Likewise, if I'm kind to my father one day, is it because of the Holy Spirit within me or because my father raised me well or because I had a good night's sleep? Again, my answer is *yes*! The convergence of these factors pulls toward life affirmation that we call the influence of the true spirit.

A person under the influence of the true spirit is in a state of consolation, which is the topic of chapter 3.

With this understanding of desolation and the false spirit and of consolation and the true spirit, the next chapters will explore the characteristics of each spirit and the state of being associated with it.

| **Desolation:** The state of being under the influence of the false spirit. | **Consolation:** The state of being under the influence of the true spirit. |

2

Characteristics of Desolation and of the False Spirit

I call desolation . . . darkness of soul, turmoil of spirit, inclination to what is low and earthly, restlessness rising from many disturbances and temptations which lead to want of faith, want of hope, want of love. The soul is wholly slothful, tepid, sad, and separated, as it were, from its Creator and Lord. For just as consolation is the opposite of desolation, so the thoughts that spring from consolation are the opposite of those that spring from desolation.

—The Spiritual Exercises of St. Ignatius*, Rules for Discernment of

Spirits, First Week, #4

Pondering those contradictory daydreams of chivalry versus religious life, Ignatius came to see that a person could determine God's will by recognizing the *source* of the movements within. When he recognized a movement as coming from the false spirit, he labeled it so and presumed it was not a movement toward God's will. When he recognized an inner movement as coming from the true spirit, he acknowledged the will of God in that movement and followed its lead. Much later in his life, after he became good at recognizing these movements, Ignatius set down in writing the characteristics of the false and true spirits and of desolation and consolation.

It would be tempting to think of desolation as feeling bad and consolation as feeling good—these definitions are close to what a dictionary

---

**The Spiritual Exercises of St. Ignatius* will hereafter be shortened to *SE.*

would give. But in Ignatian spirituality, desolation and consolation involve much more than the feelings themselves. There are times, for example, when a person is in consolation precisely *because* he or she is feeling sorrow for past sins, grief for a lost loved one, or anger for an injustice toward the poor. Likewise, the experience of desolation might actually be accompanied by feelings of happiness, comfort, or excitement.

So how do we tell the difference between desolation and consolation? Let's begin with desolation, the topic of this chapter. Here's an overview:

I am in desolation when I am empty of

- faith, hope, and love
- the sense of God's being close to me

and when I am filled with some combination of

- "disquietude" (restlessness) and agitation
- boredom and "tepidity" (apathy)
- fear and worry
- secrecy

Empty of Faith, Hope, and Love

I call desolation . . . darkness of soul . . . inclination to what is low and earthly . . . want of faith, want of hope, want of love.

—SE, RULES FOR DISCERNMENT OF SPIRITS, FIRST WEEK, #4

I know that I'm in desolation when I find myself preoccupied with the small: petty resentments, irrational worries, superficial pleasures, or low-reaching goals. When I prayerfully look back on my day (Ignatius would say, "When I pray my Examen"), I ask, "What have been the primary things on my mind and in my heart, today? What were my goals for the day?" Once I name those things that took up my time and psychic energy, I can then ask, "Did those thoughts, feelings, and goals lead me toward being a person of greater faith, hope, and love, or did they lead me away from these virtues?" These are simple questions, and by pondering them, I'll know fairly quickly which spirit has driven my day.

The examen: A quick daily reflection on the spirits that have stirred my thoughts, emotions, and actions this day.

This doesn't mean that every part of my day needs to be filled with heroic actions. Perhaps I spent the day doing housework or gardening or changing the oil in my car. I'm not asking myself how big or how heroic my actions were but rather, "Did these actions lead to greater faith, hope, and love?" For example, if I spent the day doing housework, the question would be "*Why* did I do housework? Was it out of love for my family or out of avoidance of something else I was supposed to accomplish today?" If I spent the day feeling sad about my friend's moving away, I ask myself, "Was the sadness my way of acknowledging my great love for my friend, or was it a self-indulgent refusal to get on with my life?" The movements *beneath* the thoughts, feelings, or actions will reveal the true spirit stirring me today.

Sometimes it's important to take these three virtues apart and look at them individually.

- **Faith:** Did my actions today give me greater trust in God, in the church, or in the God-given people of my life—or did they lead to unproductive and paralyzing doubts?

- **Hope:** Have the feelings I've been experiencing lately led me to greater optimism for the future and deeper confidence in God's providence—or have they led to despair and to forgetting that God will take care of me, no matter what?

- **Love:** Have the things that have preoccupied my thoughts today really led me to greater love of my neighbor—or have those thoughts coaxed me into isolation, secrecy, passivity, or aggressiveness?

Empty of the Sense of God's Closeness

I call desolation . . . [a sense of the soul's being] separated, as it were,
from its Creator and Lord.

—SE, RULES FOR DISCERNMENT OF SPIRITS, FIRST WEEK, #4

The word *desolation* has its roots in the Middle English *de sole*, which translates as "to be made alone, to be forsaken or abandoned." Part of the experience of desolation is the sense that God is distant from me. I can't feel a strong sense of God's presence. I feel spiritually abandoned and alone. I say the "sense" of God's absence or the "feeling" of being abandoned by God because faith assures me that God never abandons me. If God did so, I would cease to exist. God is always near, always watching and loving me—always acting for the good in my life. But I don't always *feel* that divine love. I can't always *sense* God's presence in my heart.

A young seminarian going through a bit of desolation described a prayer time during which he meditated on Christ as the Good Shepherd. "I found myself doubting," he said, "if I really am one of those sheep in Christ's arms." It was a strange thing for such a prayerful seminarian to say, but that's how it felt at the moment. For long periods of his life, prayer came with ease and gave him a sense of God's nearness, but at this moment of desolation he felt only an abandoned emptiness in his prayer. His words to God felt like dry bones; his petitions seemed to be unheard and unanswered. He was alone in the room, seemingly with no God to comfort him.

This unhappy sense of dryness in prayer is not unusual among people of faith. Jesus himself cried out from the cross, "My God, my God, why have you abandoned me?" The psalmist speaks of his soul as "a dry and weary land" (Psalm 63:1) and asks:

My God, my God, why have you forsaken me?
>Why are you so far from helping me, from the words of my
>>groaning?
O my God, I cry by day, but you do not answer;
>and by night, but find no rest.

—PSALM 22

St. Thérèse of Lisieux once referred to herself as an abandoned toy of the child Jesus. Mother Teresa of Calcutta endured very long stretches of prayer with no sense of the Father's presence. Frustrated by God's frequent "absences," the mystical writer Thomas à Kempis once exclaimed in prayer that if God absented himself one more time, Thomas would break every commandment in the book! These examples reveal that such an experience is normal in a life of prayer.

I am truly in the depths of desolation not simply when I experience dryness in prayer but also when I have lost the sense of hope and faith that this will ever change. In desolation, I am drawn to question not just this moment but my *entire relationship* with God. I will begin to wonder if my whole experience of God is just a sham, something I made up in my head. I will question the existence of God, or at least the existence of my friendship with God. I remember once, during a particularly dry retreat I was going through, telling my retreat director, "I'm not sure that I really know how to pray." I could tell that the director was laughing inwardly at this comment; from his more objective point of view, he knew how silly this doubt was. But in my heart the false spirit had me convinced that my years and years of prayer were nothing but an imaginative exercise—an intellectual fantasy.

Full of Disquietude and Agitation

I call desolation . . . darkness of soul, turmoil of spirit . . . restlessness rising from many disturbances and temptations.

—SE, RULES FOR DISCERNMENT OF SPIRITS, FIRST WEEK, #4

Ignatius noticed an *unsettled quality* to desolation and to the movements that came from the false spirit. He said that if a person is going "from good to better"—that is, praying and truly seeking the will of God—then the movements of the false spirit will leave her feeling uneasy, unsettled, and agitated. There will be a noticeable lack of peace in her heart. The negative feelings of fear, anger, laziness, and so on, will bother her and will seem larger than they really are. She will falsely believe that her negative emotions have got the best of her—and believing this will make it true.

Inner disturbance or restlessness—what Ignatius called disquiet—may well be the most revealing characteristic of the false spirit because it is the *disquietude about the other characteristics* that reveals its source. Note in the quotation above that Ignatius does not worry so much about "many disturbances and temptations" but rather about "*disquiet from* various agitations and temptations." There will always be agitations, negative feelings, temptations, and upsetting thoughts. What the discerner needs to pay attention to is the extent to which these negative movements within him disturb his peace of mind.

If I set out to have *no* negative moods, thoughts, or feelings, I'm setting myself up for failure. These experiences are simply part of what it means to be human. But I can pray about and work on *my perceptions of* and *attitudes toward* those negative moods, thoughts, and feelings. Often, I cannot control the way I feel about something. For example, if you say something hurtful to me, I'm going to feel hurt. Denying it will simply make it worse. But I can control my attitude about those feelings. If the hurt feelings become the driving force of my attitudes and actions—if they lead me to pessimistic conclusions about my life, and if they ultimately dictate how I act—then I am operating under the influence of the false spirit and am in desolation.

A Native American legend tells of an elder explaining to his grandson that there are two wolves within him struggling for control of his actions. One wolf is the true spirit, and the other is the false spirit. The young grandson asks, "And which will win, Grandfather?" The old man answers, "The one I feed." This is precisely the point. I do not have a choice about having the two wolves within me. This side of heaven, I must deal with inner negativity. But I do have some choice in my attitude toward that negativity.

A couple of examples might help to illustrate the point.

An Unwelcome Passenger

Recently, I took a twenty-six-hour bus trip from New Orleans to St. Joseph, Missouri. I was on my own and decided to use this trip as a time of prayer and reflection. Not long into the trip, in the midst of my prayer, I noticed the presence of a bit of anger about a past incident. The incident that elicited the anger was not very significant, and I knew, looking at it objectively, that it was not of great consequence. I therefore set out to dismiss these petty feelings of anger. But as the bus trip went on, despite my best efforts, the anger inside me grew and grew. In fact, it seemed that the more I tried to get rid of the anger, the angrier I felt.

Time went by, and the anger remained. Meanwhile, as my bus traveled from one city to another, I noticed that as I sat by the window with an empty isle seat beside me, one person would get on the bus and sit there for a while and then would get off at the next stop; then another would sit in that seat, then another, and so on. With one person I might have a lengthy and friendly conversation, and with another there might be silence the entire time. With some amusement I thought, *I feel like I'm having fifty first dates, each of them lasting about three hundred miles!*

Meanwhile, I began to realize that my anger just wasn't going away. I prayed some more about this and suddenly found myself speaking directly to my anger: "OK, anger, it seems as though I can't get you off the bus. I suppose that you insist on being one of my dates. So, I consent to your staying around a while. You can stay and sit beside me quietly while I pray, as long as you don't make too much noise and as long as you don't try to sit in the driver's seat." True to form, like my other dates, anger sat beside me for about three hundred miles and then, on its own, got off the bus.

"Agitations" will come and go in life. I can't stop them from coming. And often, when I make great efforts to kick them off the bus, they simply become more obstinate. Because I focus all my attention on them, they have now moved into the driver's seat. But if I allow the good spirit of Peace and Quiet to *drive* the bus, it isn't so distressing that Anger is a fellow passenger.

Here is another example of how the false spirit sometimes attempts to let the "agitations and temptations" rule a person's life and bring about disquietude.

A Case of Righteous Anger

I once counseled a troubled young man named Frank, who seldom smiled and who had few friends. Early in my pastoral counseling sessions with him, he began to let loose pent-up feelings about his being victimized years before. In these early sessions, Frank had the liberating experience of finally acknowledging what had happened to him and how it made him feel. He was filled with righteous anger—that is, anger that he had a right to—and expressing this anger out loud for the first time (as opposed to repressing it as he'd always done before) brought him some peace and satisfaction. I was pleased and knew that these "controlled explosions" in the safety of my office were from the true spirit.

But as the weeks went on, I noticed that Frank was not letting go of that anger. Instead, he was *feeding and being fed by his anger*. It was anger that got him out of bed in the morning and anger that led to his brooding silences among his peers at school.

I began to recognize two opposing movements within Frank. Acknowledging and expressing his anger in a spiritual context was coming from the true spirit. Disquiet about that same anger was coming from the false spirit. In order for Frank to follow the path of the true spirit, he would have to find ways of accepting the past event and his present feelings about the event. But he would also have to come to peace within himself about his present emotions. He would have to consent to having anger as a passenger on the bus without allowing the anger to drive the bus.

Confusion: A Subcategory

Confusion is such a common experience within desolation that we might be tempted to think of it as a distinct characteristic of desolation. But confusion in and of itself is not the problem. God never promises us certainty; omniscience belongs to God alone. Most of the time, a healthy discernment process will go through one or more periods of ambiguity and uncertainty. In fact, this is often a necessary stage in the course of good discernment. The problem, then, is with our reaction to this lack of clarity. Confusion becomes a desolating experience when we allow ourselves to be upset about not knowing—when our uncertainty or lack of knowledge leads to disturbance within us.

Nonetheless, unsettling confusion is indeed a common telltale sign of desolation. A person in this state is missing the forest for the trees. He loses his perspective of the ultimate goal of life, which is defined by St. Ignatius as "praise, reverence, and service of God our Lord." The confusion of desola-

> John Kavanaugh asked Mother Theresa to pray for him to have clarity. She said, "I've never had clarity and certitude. I only have trust. I'll pray that you trust."

tion causes a person to get bogged down in the details of the journey while forgetting the ultimate destination. It's a failure to "keep your eyes on the prize." Otherwise, the state of not knowing would not be unsettling and therefore not desolating.

Consider the story of Peter walking on the water to meet Jesus. As long as Peter was focused on Jesus, he walked with ease. If he were asked at that moment, "How is it that you are walking on water?" he would not know the answer. But his lack of understanding about water walking did not keep him from doing so, as long as he focused on Jesus. It was upon "seeing the wind" that Peter grew afraid and began to sink. The moment he took his eyes off Jesus, he was lost.

Immediately he made the disciples get into the boat and go on ahead to the other side, while he dismissed the crowds. And after he had dismissed the crowds, he went up the mountain by himself to pray. When evening came, he was there alone, but by this time the boat, battered by the waves, was far from the land, for the wind was against them. And early in the morning he came walking toward them on the sea. But when the disciples saw him walking on the sea, they were terrified, saying, "It is a ghost!" And they cried out in fear. But immediately Jesus spoke to them and said, "Take heart, it is I; do not be afraid."

Peter answered, "Lord, if it is you, command me to come to you on the water." He said, "Come!" So Peter got out of the boat, started walking on the water, and came toward Jesus. But when he noticed the strong wind, he became frightened, and beginning to sink, he cried out, "Lord, save me!" Jesus immediately reached out his hand and caught him, saying to him, "You of little faith, why did you doubt?" (Matthew 14:22–31)

Full of Boredom and Tepidity

I call desolation . . . wholly slothful, tepid.

—SE, RULES FOR DISCERNMENT OF SPIRITS, FIRST WEEK, #4

In desolation, I may be experiencing not disquiet and agitation but rather boredom and apathy—or, in the words of Ignatius, tepidity. Contrary to popular belief, hate is not the opposite of love. When I hate someone, at least I am engaged in that person's life. I am in relationship with him. I have allowed that person to move me, to change me. The opposite of love is apathy, whereby I don't care about the person enough to hate him. I am most unloving when you mean so little to me that I feel nothing for you at all.

> I wish that you were either cold or hot. So, because you are luke-warm, and neither cold nor hot, I am about to spit you out of my mouth. (Revelation 3:15–16)

As a counselor or a spiritual director, there is much I can do to work with a person who feels hatred, even hatred toward God. Such strong feelings indicate that you are wrestling, struggling in relationship. We can use this passion! We can approach God with it and allow God to do what needs to be done for healing. But if a person is apathetic, there is little that a mentor can do to help. There is no engagement, no relationship. The most that one can do is to name the apathy and try to move out of it. Until then, the person is a sailboat lost on a windless sea.

Earlier I pointed out that the experience of feeling distant from God is a strong sign of desolation. Worse yet is the lack of *desire* to be close to Christ. This, too, is a more common experience for believers than you might think. Even strong, faith-filled Christians go through times when they don't feel like praying, they don't want to go to church, and they resist spiritual renewal. I remember talking to my spiritual director about the absence of God I felt in my prayer.

"Do you *want* God to be close?" she asked.

I thought it was a silly question for a nun to ask a seminarian and answered by telling her about my devotion to my vocation, my faithfulness to prayer, and so on. She asked a second time, "Do you *desire* to be close to God, right now?"

Again I obfuscated by giving lofty statements about faith and fortitude. She patiently listened with a loving, nonjudgmental smile and, only when I was finished, asked a third time, "Mark, do you *desire* to be close to Jesus?"

I leaned back in the chair, closed my eyes, and breathed deeply. "No," I said, to my great surprise.

"OK," she said, "That's OK. Now we can get to work."

Just as hate is not the opposite of love, so too, death is not the opposite of life. Death is a stage of life—a portal to new life. When I am dying, literally or figuratively, I am still on life's spectrum. If life were a mountain, dying would be the descent down the mountain—which could be happy or sad, natural or unnatural. The opposite of life, then, is not death but tepidity, tediousness, boredom, blandness, indifference, lethargy. None of these feelings is from the true spirit. In the spiritual life, St. Ignatius found this state far more distressing than the state of being at odds with God or agitated by spiritual disruptions. From my brother who sails I've learned that I can use any wind, from any direction, to get my sailboat back home. But if there is no wind at all, there is little that can be done.

Full of Fear and Worry

A thorough reading of the Gospels would reveal that perhaps the most persistent command from God is not about sex or violence or a lack of religious practice but rather about not being afraid. In the Nativity stories of Matthew's and Luke's Gospels alone, it is staggering how many people are told not to be afraid—practically every character in the story!

- Mary is told, "Do not be afraid, Mary, for you have found favor with God." (Luke 1:30)
- Joseph is told, "Do not be afraid to take Mary as your wife." (Matthew 1:20)
- Zacharias is told, "Do not be afraid, Zechariah, for your prayer has been heard. Your wife Elizabeth will bear you a son." (Luke 1:13)
- In turn, Zechariah, filled with the Holy Spirit, proclaims that God is visiting his people so that we "might serve him without fear." (Luke 1:74)
- The shepherds are told, "Do not be afraid; for see—I am bringing you good news of great joy." (Luke 2:10)

In each of these cases it seems that fear is the biggest obstacle to these good people's carrying out God's will. In fact, no other obstacle is mentioned. All this in the first two chapters of the Gospels! Throughout the Gospels, we see the effects of fear:

- Fear keeps Herod from rejoicing in the newborn Savior.
- Fear keeps Nicodemus from following Christ in the light of day.
- Fear keeps the Pharisees from dealing straightforwardly with Jesus.
- Fear keeps the disciples from recognizing Jesus walking on the water.
- Fear keeps Peter from walking on water.

- Fear leads the apostles to abandon Jesus when he is arrested.
- Fear keeps Peter from admitting his friendship with Jesus.
- Fear keeps the women at the empty tomb from proclaiming that Jesus has risen.

Far more often than we'd like to admit, fear is the motivation behind our actions. We are afraid of losing friendships, of losing our jobs, of getting hurt, of failing, of disappointing others, of facing the truth, and of looking stupid. We fear our bosses, our neighbors, our leaders, and sometimes even our friends and family. Most of all we fear ourselves: our unreflected-upon emotions and our secret desires, our strongest attractions and our deepest repulsions. This fear, it seems, is the true motivation behind our actions and our failures to act. Otherwise, why would the Gospels harp on it so much?

St. Ignatius says that for a person sincerely trying to find God's will, fear is not a tool of the true spirit. When fear is in our hearts, chances are, we are not focused on what God is saying to us.

Later on, I will define consolation as letting God dream in me. If that is the case, then desolation is allowing the false spirit to nightmare in me. I am in desolation when I become preoccupied by false futures of impending doom. I become convinced that, just around the corner, things will go badly for me. Rather than remain in the present, I dwell on frightening possibilities that will never happen.

I remember counseling a virtuous and smart teenager who was caught cheating. "You're so intelligent," I said to him. "Why did you do it?"

"Because I'm scared that I'm going to fail the class," he answered. And sure enough, I saw the fear in his eyes.

"Well, let's look at the evidence," I said. "Have you ever failed a class before?"

"No."

"Did you fail this class last quarter?"

"No."

"Has the teacher warned you that you're going to fail this quarter?"

"No."

"What grade did you make in this class last quarter?"

"B−."

"Well then, why on earth would you think that you'll go from a B− to an F?"

Realization came at that moment, and finally he was able to breathe. "Yeah, you're right. I'm not going to fail."

> O Christ Jesus,
> When all is darkness
> And we feel our weakness and
>   helplessness,
> Give us the sense of Your presence,
> Your love, and Your strength.
> Help us to have perfect trust
> In Your protecting love
> And strengthening power,
> So that nothing may frighten or
>   worry us,
> For, living close to You,
> We shall see Your hand,
> Your purpose, Your will through all
>   things.
>   —ST. IGNATIUS OF LOYOLA,
>   ATTRIBUTED

I once lived with an older priest who had had a difficult childhood growing up during the Great Depression of the 1930s. Often at lunchtime he would eat only a small amount of what was on his plate, and then he would walk to his bedroom and set the plate of food down on a bookshelf. Usually he would not return to the food, and it would have to be thrown out. When I wondered about this odd behavior, someone pointed out to me that people who have gone through a traumatic experience of hunger have unconscious fears of running out of food. They often need to keep food within sight, close by them, in order to calm their fears. I've heard of Holocaust survivors, for example, waking up in a panic in the middle of the night and calming themselves simply by turning on the pantry light and looking at the canned foods. The older priest's habit of keeping his lunch on the bookshelf is a good metaphor for what fear does to everyone: it causes us to hoard things, people, emotions, and our own gifts and talents rather than relish and share them. The gift hoarded and unused goes bad and must be thrown away.

If we take an honest look at the mistakes we've made, we'll see that many of them were a reaction to unnamed fear within us. Psychology teaches that even anger is often a mask for fear. When we are angry, we should ask ourselves, *In what way do I feel threatened right now?* and we will learn the true source of our emotional outbursts.

The fears we have aren't always so dramatic; sometimes they exhibit themselves as worry about the next moment. I remember once planning to go to an event with one of my brother Jesuits. I decided to dress casually for it, but I became worried that my companion that evening would dress up. With absolutely no basis in reality, I became convinced that he would be irritated with me for dressing down and would say something judgmental. The more I imagined this confrontation, the angrier I became. Being the sharp-minded and sharp-witted Jesuit that I am, I thought of some quick retorts that I could use to lash back at him. Well, you know the end of this story: when I walked to his room, there he was, more casually dressed than I!

Not all fears are bad. Healthy fear moves me to lock my doors at night and to wisely keep my mouth shut when I don't know what I'm talking about. Note that in the previous examples, it is the *irrational* nature of these fears that reveal that they are not from the true spirit.

But desolation can use even rational fears to stop me from acting boldly toward the good I'm called to do. In the Gospel Nativity stories, Joseph's fears of taking Mary for his wife were well founded. It's easy to imagine the trouble he would have to endure for marrying a pregnant girl in first-century Palestine. Joseph had good reason to fear. But even rational fear shouldn't be the driver of the bus. God sometimes calls me to do things that are genuinely frightening, and in those situations it's natural to be afraid. But I can choose not to *feed* and *be fed by* that fear. Rather, I can choose to act boldly, trusting in the promise that God will take care of those who follow his will.

Full of Secrecy

Before his conversion, it seems that St. Ignatius spent a lot of time seducing young girls and married women. Looking back on that embarrassing period, he used it as a metaphor for the way the false spirit seduces us all:

> *[The false spirit] seeks to remain hidden and does not want to be discovered. If such a lover speaks with evil intention to the daughter of a good father or to the wife of a good husband, and seeks to seduce them, he wants his words and solicitations kept secret. . . . In the same way, when the enemy of our human nature tempts a just soul with his wiles and seductions, he earnestly desires that they be received secretly and kept secret. But if one manifests them to a confessor, or to some other spiritual person who understands his deceits and malicious designs . . . his evident deceits have been revealed.*
>
> —SE, Rules for Discernment of Spirits, First Week, #13

Ignatius warns against the false spirit's trick of getting me to keep things secret from my mentors and companions. Common sense requires that I not tell everyone everything all the time. However, if my companions and mentors are well chosen and are trustworthy, there is virtually no reason to keep any part of my inner life secret from them. If I find myself doing so, chances are, the false spirit is afoot. When I am in desolation, I cannot trust my own judgment; I will need the objectivity and sensibility of the wise and loving people around me. Otherwise, I will be lost in my own private fog and will not even be aware of the fog's existence. The spirit of desolation will attempt to leave me in this fog by keeping me from those who are standing outside it. I will convince myself that

- He wouldn't understand.
- She'll overreact.
- We don't have time to talk about it now.
- It's not that important anyhow.

- It's too embarrassing to mention.
- He'll be ashamed of me. It will disappoint him.
- I need to work this out before I tell her about it.
- I'll deal with it later—it can wait.
- It will resolve itself.
- He's too busy to be bothered with this.
- She's dealing with her own personal issues right now.
- I know what she'll say.
- He'll be hurt . . . angry . . . disappointed.
- She's too old fashioned . . . liberal . . . judgmental to understand.

If I find myself using these reasons to keep something from my mentors and companions, then I should take it as a sign that desolation is trying to preserve itself. I should not delay in telling my mentors and companions the *whole* story, leaving out no details.

For example, it is quite common for a religious novice to gradually convince himself that a problem he's currently having is a sign from God that he is not called to religious life after all. Being a novice, he will not be aware that the problem is either fixable or manageable and certainly not grounds for leaving. But the false spirit will convince the novice that he needs to work out this discernment for himself rather than discuss it with the novice director. The novice will become convinced that, while it is normally vital to be completely transparent to his elders, his particular situation is a special case. The spirit of desolation will quietly feed the novice one false notion after another, building a stronger and stronger case for the novice to leave, all the while keeping this entire discernment secret. The novice will not approach the novice director until he has firmly decided to leave. Sometimes he will have already purchased a plane ticket or called a family member to drive over to pick him up. The false spirit will have arranged it such that it is too late for the novice director to stop the train; it is already careering off the track.

False Consolation:
An Advanced Form of Desolation

In his writings on discernment of spirits, St. Ignatius spoke of a particular kind of desolation that comes in the life of a spiritually more advanced person. **False consolation** is the experience of being drawn to feelings, thoughts, and motivations that look good and holy at first but that ultimately lead to actions to which God is not calling that person, or not calling that person to at that time.

In the words of Ignatius, the false spirit at time will

> *assume the appearance of an angel of light. He begins by suggesting thoughts that are suited to a devout soul, and ends by suggesting his own. For example, he will suggest holy and pious thoughts that are wholly in conformity with the sanctity of the soul. Afterward, he will endeavor little by little to end by drawing the soul into his hidden snares and evil designs.*
> —*SE*, Rules for Discernment of Spirits, Second Week, #4

Once a Christian has begun to take her faith seriously—to pray, to attend church, to seek spiritual advice, and so on—she is not so tempted by blatant sin. Generally speaking, she is not as attracted by unloving acts, self-destructive behaviors, sexual promiscuity, and so on. For such a person, temptations may begin to come in the form of attractions to *holy* distractions that would keep her from her particular callings from God.

There's the story of a friendly little western town that had no church bell in the steeple. The impoverished townsfolk had no clocks or watches and had no idea of when the Mass might begin, so they all came to the churchyard early on Sunday morning and sat around and visited with one another until the start of Mass.

Then one day, the devil, in the guise of a rich benefactor, came to the town and donated a church bell. The townsfolk were elated and profusely thanked this "holy man" who had given such a great gift. Now, every Sunday, the church bell rang a few minutes before the start of Mass. There was no longer any need to go early and therefore all that early morning community-building time in the churchyard suddenly ceased to be.

God has a particular calling for each person; we are not called to do every holy action that comes to mind or to respond to every good opportunity. For example, I can't join ongoing relief efforts on the ground in Haiti and teach freshmen in a Catholic school in America. I must choose which of these good callings God intends for me. False consolation is the experience of feeling as though I am in consolation when, in reality, I am moving away from what God's plan is for me at this time.

A great example of this is the experience of Jesus himself as told in Matthew's Gospel. In chapter 14, Jesus miraculously turns a few loaves of bread into enough to feed thousands of people. So for Jesus to miraculously make bread is a good and holy thing, right? But what about earlier, in Matthew 4, when Jesus was being tempted in the wilderness? There, Jesus *resisted* the urge to make bread miraculously. Why would he resist?

> Jesuit father Jean Pierre de Caussade said that the finest bread is as poison to the one not called to eat it and the vilest poison is as the finest bread to the person who is called to eat it.

Making bread appears at first glance to be a good and holy thing. Bread, after all, was destined to be an important instrument in Jesus' ministry. So why did Jesus resist so vehemently? He resisted because he knew that the *source* of his attraction to making bread at that particular moment of his life was not of the true spirit. This holy attraction was not rooted in the stirrings of the Father and would not have drawn Jesus closer to the Father.

> Then Jesus was led up by the Spirit into the wilderness to be tempted by the devil. He fasted forty days and forty nights, and afterwards he was famished. The tempter came and said to him, "If you are the Son of God, command these stones to become loaves of bread." But he answered, "It is written, 'One does not live by bread alone, but by every word that comes from the mouth of God.'" (Matthew 4:1–4)

Another good example is from my own life experience. For nine years I taught and ministered at two Jesuit high schools in Texas. They were some of the happiest years of my life. I know that it was God who sent me to this ministry and who graced my life and work. Gratitude was one of the strongest, most prevalent graces that I found myself bringing to Christ in prayer at this time.

However, all through those years, I was troubled by a notion that I should be ministering to the destitute out in the missions somewhere. I say "troubled" because it was not so much a great desire as much as a feeling of guilt for all the things I had in life. I felt guilty for being happy and guilty for having a comfortable home and three square meals a day. I also felt guilty for "wasting" my precious young priesthood on the wealthy rather than on the poor. As will be explained later in the book, this guilt, as opposed to desire, was a strong indication that it was not from the true spirit. Knowing this and discussing it with various friends and mentors through the years, I made a conscious choice not to act on those "holy" urgings to drop everything and go to the missions. Still, the thoughts and feelings persisted and never left me throughout the years of my teaching assignment.

False consolation: The experience of being drawn to feelings, thoughts, and actions that look good and holy at first but ultimately lead to actions that the person is not called by God to do at this time.

Finally, the time came for me to finish my second tenure in Jesuit high school work and to move on to tertianship, which is an internal ongoing formation experience for Jesuits who have been in the Society for many years. As part of the formation experience, I had the opportunity to spend more than four months in practically any ministry opportunity in the world. Knowing this notion of the missions had disturbed my happy life during all those years of high school work, I asked to work with some of the poorest people in the world: the Sudanese refugees living in exile in "the bush" of northern Uganda.

Those four months were a life-changing experience for me. God taught me many lessons through getting to know those beautiful, war-weary people. One person with whom I became friends was Azay, a twenty-year-old refugee living in a mud-and-thatch hut not far from the Jesuit Refugee Service compound where I lived. Azay's extraordinary story was actually quite ordinary among the young refugee men of the area. When Azay was about nine years old, the Sudanese rebel army came to his village and demanded that each household give up one boy to fight with them in their ongoing war with the government. Facing certain death for the entire family, Azay's parents handed him over to the army. Azay has not seen them since. In the beginning, his little arms were too weak to lift a rifle, so he was made an indentured servant for the commanders. Later, as he grew bigger, he was made a soldier in this war he knew nothing of and wanted no part in. One day, when in his early teens, Azay and several of his fellow boy soldiers escaped from the army. This escape led to years and years of crossing deserts and crocodile-infested rivers in several countries. Eventually, he ended up in northern Uganda, built his little mud hut with one of his friends, and settled down as best he could.

But I have not yet mentioned the most remarkable part of the story: Azay happened to be one of the happiest people I've ever met! He was kind and prayerful, industrious and funny. He smiled all the time and sang praise songs to Jesus all day. He was quite a businessman, wheeling and dealing in his carpentry service and chicken farm. He was good looking and had healthy friendships with people of all ages. This guy had it all together!

Meanwhile, once a week, I would travel an hour and a half to "town" to shop and run other errands. Checking my e-mail at the Internet café, I received updates on Billy, a former student of mine from Dallas who was having some sort of psychological and spiritual meltdown. Week by week the news got worse, until finally Billy was placed in a treatment center, where he languished for quite a while. Billy's past could not be more different from Azay's. He grew up in a wealthy American family and was deeply loved and cared for. He went to the best schools, took exciting vacations, and was active at church and in Boy Scouts. He had the perfect American upbringing.

Azay and Billy were about the same age, so it isn't surprising that, in my musings, I often compared these two different lives. One day, wondering at the pure joy of this destitute African and the misery of this wealthy American, I heard Jesus ask me, *Mark, which of these two young men needs a priest more? Which is more impoverished?*

> Every day you have to say yes. Total surrender! To be where He wants you to be. . . . If God wants you to be in a palace, alright . . . accept to be in the palace.
>
> —MOTHER TERESA OF CALCUTTA

Through these and other experiences, I gradually received the grace to let go of the guilt that distracted me from giving my all to the boys at our Jesuit high schools. Finally, the false spirit dressed in the angelic robes of an African missionary revealed its true identity. I came back to the United States a different person, ready to accept whatever God would call me to next, regardless of how many seemingly holier alternatives beckoned from the false spirit.

Here are a few less dramatic examples of how the false spirit might appear as an angel of light:

- A young woman enters the convent not because she feels called to it but because she thinks it is a holier life, a more perfect life, than motherhood.
- A mother is overly harsh as she pushes her son to make good grades.
- A father smothers his daughter with attention and gifts, and she never grows up.
- A middle-aged man abandons his family because he has fallen in love with a woman who "really understands me for who I am."
- The friend of an alcoholic becomes obsessed with "fixing" him.
- A young Catholic college student fails to turn in an important paper because she has spent all her time prepping for the next Catholic Center retreat.

In sum, a good Christian might be in false consolation when he is attracted to something holy that happens to be

- the wrong mission for this particular person
- the right mission but the wrong timing
- the right mission but with the wrong method, emphasis, or degree of involvement.

The Combination of Characteristics

Having looked at the various characteristics of the false spirit, we can see that it is usually the combination of these characteristics that constitutes the experience of desolation. Take for example an elderly woman who is lonely and bored in an empty house and would like to go to the community center to see her friends. Since she has no means of transportation, she considers telling her son about her desires but decides not to (*secrecy*). "It is unchristian to make myself a burden to others (*bad thoughts disguised as angels of light*). Besides, if I bother my son too much, he'll start to resent it and will stop coming to visit me" (*irrational worry over the future*).

It may well be that the son greatly desires to be more active in his mother's life. It could be that the son is aware that the community center provides free transportation but is unaware of his mother's desire to go. Perhaps Christ is calling the woman to be more sociable, and it is he who has placed in her this desire to go to the community center, but the false spirit has convinced her that it is unchristian to express one's desires.

These combinations of characteristics produce the effect of closing the self in and of keeping God and loved ones at arm's length.

3

Characteristics of Consolation and of the True Spirit

It is characteristic of the good spirit, however, to give courage and strength, consolations, tears, inspirations, and peace. This He does by making all easy, by removing all obstacles so that the soul goes forward in doing good.

—*SE*, Rules for Discernment of Spirits, First Week, #2

The characteristics of consolation are generally opposite the characteristics of desolation. If desolation is the state of lacking faith, hope, and love, then consolation is an abundance of those virtues. If fear usually accompanies desolation, then courage usually accompanies consolation. And so on.

I call it consolation when an interior movement is aroused in the soul, by which it is inflamed with love of its Creator and Lord, and as a consequence, can love no creature on the face of the earth for its own sake, but only in the Creator of them all. It is likewise consolation when one sheds tears that move to the love of God, whether it be because of sorrow for sins, or because of the sufferings of Christ our Lord, or for any other reason that is immediately directed to the praise and service of God. Finally, I call consolation every increase of faith, hope, and love, and all interior joy that invites and attracts to what is heavenly and to the salvation of one's soul by filling it with peace and quiet in its Creator and Lord.

—*SE*, Rules for Discernment of Spirits, First Week, #3

It takes years to understand the crucial subtleties of these experiences and to depart from the misconception that consolation is about feeling good and desolation is about feeling bad.

I am in consolation when I have

- faith, hope, and love
- the sense of God's closeness
- peace and tranquility
- great desires
- transparency.

Faith, Hope, and Love

I call consolation every increase of faith, hope, and love.

—*SE*, Rules for Discernment of Spirits, First Week, #3

The "increase of faith, hope, and love" is placed first on my list of characteristics because it and the next one (the sense of God's closeness) are the greatest telltale signs of desolation or consolation. Consider the famous "love passage" of 1 Corinthians 13: "If I speak in the tongues of mortals and of angels, but do not have love, I am a noisy gong or a clanging cymbal." My spiritual life may be cluttered with holy thoughts and clever insights. I may be filled up with warm fuzzy feelings and may have discovered new gifts and talents within me. But if these thoughts, feelings, and talents are not increasing my faith, hope, and love, then what good are they?

Or I may be feeling down in the dumps today. I may have failed miserably at some task. I may be confused about where I am in life or angry about something that has happened. But if my anger motivates me to push for justice or truth, if my confusion leads me to trust in God more than in myself, if my failure or sadness leads me to reach out to the people in my life, then perhaps these negative experiences aren't so negative after all.

Clare was a kindhearted, easygoing young woman who struggled with passivity. For various reasons, she found it difficult to be proactive and assertive in her Christian callings. While doing an Ignatian retreat, she felt called to experience inwardly the trauma of Jesus' suffering and death. In the midst of this experience, she stormed into the director's office one day and sharply described the "absurdity" of Jesus' passion. "This should not have happened," she said, fury in her voice. "He didn't do anything wrong!" As the retreat continued, this anger over the injustice of Christ's passion resulted in a strong desire to act—to do something about the absurd injustices Clare encountered in her own life.

If I speak with the tongues of men and of angels, but do not have love, I have become a noisy gong or a clanging cymbal. If I have the gift of prophecy, and know all mysteries and all knowledge; and if I have all faith, so as to remove mountains, but do not have love, I am nothing. And if I give all my possessions to feed the poor, and if I surrender my body to be burned, but do not have love, it profits me nothing. But now faith, hope, love, abide these three; but the greatest of these is love.

Marty was a devout young priest who wanted badly to be close to Christ but who struggled with spiritual pride, taking a bit too much credit for his accomplishments and apparent holiness. When he approached the moment of praying over Christ's passion, he felt nothing at all at first. Then he felt frustration at his inability to feel anything as he watched Christ suffer for him. As the retreat went on, the frustration turned to self-loathing, so much so that by the end of that phase of the retreat, Marty was no longer focused on Jesus at all but rather on his own seemingly cold heart.

Was Clare in desolation or consolation? How about Marty? We would need more information to know for sure, but the descriptions indicate consolation for Clare and desolation for Marty. Why? It is because Clare's anger toward the injustice of the cross led her to act more lovingly toward the persecuted people in her own life. The feelings seemed to lead to an *increase of love.* However, while one might think that Marty's self-loathing would lessen his pride, it actually seemed to increase his attention on himself. He let go of his self-centered pride in exchange for self-centered self-loathing. As the retreat progressed for him, there was no outward reach toward Jesus or toward others. This self-loathing further confirms the presence of pride in his life, because instead of recognizing that this compassion must come as a grace from God, Marty still subconsciously believed that he must generate compassion for Jesus' suffering. There seems to be a *decrease of faith and of love.*

If the false spirit has me confused and disoriented, I can often cut through the confusion and mess by asking myself in prayer, *What is the most loving thing to do? What is the most hopeful thing to do? What is the most faith-filled thing to do?* Once a younger brother Jesuit publicly confronted me about numerous ways in which I irritated him. I listened quietly and said little at the time, preferring instead to think and pray before responding. During the next few days, I came to believe that some of his complaints about me were justifiable and some were not. Of the points with which I agreed, I committed myself to admit to him my need for change and to promise to work on them. I disagreed with some of his other points, however, and felt that integrity and honesty obliged me to tell him this as well.

The problem was that my wounded pride led me to fantasize about telling him off or about saying something hurtful to him. How do I express my disagreements without letting my hurt and anger seek revenge? Knowing that the true spirit comes in love, I prepared for the meeting by asking myself in prayer, *What is the most loving thing to say to him? What is the most loving way to say it?* After apologizing to him for the wrongs, I tried to confront him about our points of disagreement, but only in ways that would actually help him grow. It was a great conversation that actually strengthened our friendship.

The Sense of God's Closeness

I call it consolation when an interior movement is aroused in the soul,
by which it is inflamed with love of its Creator and Lord, and as a
consequence, can love no creature on the face of the earth for its own
sake, but only in the Creator of them all.

—SE, Rules for Discernment of Spirits, First Week, #3

One of the strongest signs of consolation is the strong, deep, and lasting sense of God's presence. It's not enough simply to believe that God exists and that God is good. Deep in the soul, we have *experienced* God's presence and God's *personal* love for us. This is an intimacy in which God seems to be gazing at us directly and specifically. "By name I have called you," says God through the prophet Isaiah:

> But now thus says the Lord,
>> he who created you, O Jacob,
>> he who formed you, O Israel:
> "Do not fear, for I have redeemed you;
>> I have called you by name, you are mine.

—Isaiah 43:1

When a person is in consolation, she reads those words and knows them to be true because of the nearness of God in her heart. "I *am* God's!" the consoled proclaims with awe and wonder.

While the experience of feeling uniquely loved by God often begins in the intimacy of private prayer, it never remains private. When the person of prayer returns to his ordinary life, he recognizes and reverences God's love for him in every object, person, or event. There suddenly exists a fourth dimension in the universe—a newly found reality of God's personal love singing in the stillness and in the action of creation, in the solidity of the tree and in the fury of the thunderstorm. Ignatius put it this way:

> [I bring to memory] the blessings of creation and redemption, and the special favors I have received. I will ponder with great affection how much God our Lord has done for me, and how much He has given me of what He possesses, and finally, how much, as far as He can, the same Lord desires to give Himself to me according to His divine decrees. . . . [Second Point] This is to reflect how God dwells in creatures: in the elements giving them existence, in the plants giving them life, in the animals conferring upon them sensation, in man bestowing understanding. So He dwells in me and gives me being, life, sensation, intelligence; and makes a temple of me, since I am created in the likeness and image of the Divine Majesty. [Third Point] This is to consider how God works and labors for me in all creatures upon the face of the earth, that is, He conducts Himself as one who labors. Thus, in the heavens, the elements, the plants, the fruits, the cattle, etc., He gives being, conserves them, confers life and sensation, etc. . . . [Fourth Point] This is to consider all blessings and gifts as descending from above. Thus, my limited power comes from the supreme and infinite power above, and so, too, justice, goodness, mercy, etc., descend from above as the rays of light descend from the sun, and as the waters flow from their fountains.
>
> —SE, Contemplation to Attain the Love of God, pp. 101–103

Once we have experienced such love in all creation, it is impossible to love creation with merely a human love. The person in consolation "can love no creature on the face of the earth for its own sake," says Ignatius, "but only in the Creator of them all." The consoled do not simply love creation, people, and things—they love God, who is laboring in all those things.

This divine love communicated between God's presence in me and God's presence in creation leads me to a transcendent synchronicity with creation. The rhythm of the universe pulses in sync with the primal pulse of my heart. I sense the pulse of God in all of it: first in my heart, then in birdsong, silent leaf, crying baby, and yes, even in idling car engine and droning refrigerator. It's all God's pulse—everywhere and in everything. In all these ordinary and mundane ways, says St. Ignatius, the good spirit's action is "delicate, gentle, delightful. It may be compared to a drop of water penetrating a sponge." The sweetness and holiness of the universe, despite all humankind's bungling of them, enter my heart "as one coming into his own house when the doors are open" (Rules, Second Week, #7).

> Chance is perhaps the pseudonym of God when he does not wish to sign his work.
> —ANATOLE FRANCE

On a more pragmatic level, this divine syncopation sometimes reveals itself in what the secular world calls coincidence but the faith-filled community calls providence. God uses chance and random happenings to communicate with us. I remember recently feeling called to do my annual retreat at a monastery rather than at the more usual Jesuit retreat house. But which monastery? I mulled it over for several weeks without a strong sense of direction. In fact, I felt a pull toward holding off on a decision and waiting for God to let me know. Then, one day, a brother Jesuit put in my mailbox a recent newspaper clipping lauding the hospitality of a particular Benedictine monastery called Conception Abbey. I took it as a sign and explored the possibility further. Months later, I found myself there having one of the best retreats of my life.

Peace and Tranquility

It is characteristic of the good spirit, however, to give courage and strength, consolations, tears, inspirations, and peace. This He does by making all easy, by removing all obstacles so that the soul goes forward in doing good.

—SE, R*ULES FOR* D*ISCERNMENT OF* S*PIRITS*, F*IRST* W*EEK*, #2

I call consolation . . . filling [the soul] with peace and quiet in its Creator and Lord.

—R*ULES*, F*IRST* W*EEK*, #3

The previous chapter explained that Ignatius is concerned not so much with "agitations and temptations," which he knows are sure to come, but with "*disquiet from* various agitations and temptations." In a similar vein, the peace and tranquility that accompany consolation are not to be understood as the absence of problems and negative emotions. This is an unrealistic expectation. The peace of consolation is not peace "as the world gives" (John 14:27), which is merely the state of no conflict. Rather, the peace of consolation is the state of being at peace specifically about the various agitations and temptations of my life. This peace isn't a peace *without* problems, agitations, and so on. It isn't even peace *despite* problems. It is a divine peace *about* those difficult, unresolved issues of my life. I know that I have problems. I'm fully aware of the unpleasant and unredeemed aspects of my life. I may on the surface feel terribly upset, angry, or sad about them. But I have a sense *deeper down* that God is *working through* even these difficult parts of my life. I have a sense that just as God can transform a reprehensible thing like public execution into a means of salvation, God can transform any and every reprehensible part of my life, too. The tranquility of consolation is the assurance not only that God will save me *from* the problems of my life (self-inflicted or otherwise) but also that

51

God will save me *through* these problems. Only an assurance such as this can give me true peace.

A more careful reading of the Gospel Resurrection stories displays this noneuphoric peace of consolation. A businesslike evaluation of the Resurrection would have us believe that the Resurrection was not all that successful. All the problems of the early Christian community before the Resurrection seem to remain after the Resurrection: Martha still clings too much; Thomas still doubts; the disciples still flee and hide from their vocations; Peter stubbornly clings to his need to control; and priests, scholars, and government leaders still conspire with lies and false accusations. With all these problems still present, what *was* the purpose of the Resurrection? What has changed? Where is this peace that Christ promised?

Acts of the Apostles has the answer:

Now when [the Pharisees] saw the boldness of Peter and John and realized that they were uneducated and ordinary men, they were amazed and recognized them as companions of Jesus. . . . [They] ordered them not to speak or teach at all in the name of Jesus. But Peter and John answered them, "Whether it is right in God's sight to listen to you rather than to God, you must judge; for we cannot keep from speaking about what we have seen and heard." . . .

Someone arrived and announced [to the Pharisees], "Look! The men whom you put in prison are standing in the temple and teaching the people!" . . . The high priest questioned them, saying, "We gave you strict orders not to teach in this name, yet here you have filled Jerusalem with your teaching and you are determined to bring this man's blood on us." But Peter and the apostles answered, "We must obey God rather than any human authority." . . . When [the Pharisees] heard this, they were enraged and wanted to kill them. . . . They had them flogged. Then they ordered them not to speak in the name of Jesus, and let them go. As they left the council, they rejoiced that they were considered worthy to suffer dishonor for the sake of the name. And every day in the temple and at home they did not cease to teach and proclaim Jesus as the Messiah. (Acts 4:13–20; 5:25–42)

This account reveals all the signs of consolation. Peter, the one who before the Resurrection was too afraid simply to admit that he knew Jesus, finds himself talking incessantly about him—despite threats, beatings, and incarceration. Despite retaining the limitations of their past (the writer reminds us that they were "uneducated and untrained men"), the "boldness of Peter and John" amazed and paralyzed the Pharisees.

Looking at this peace and tranquility from another angle, we could call this characteristic of consolation *courage* as opposed to the paralyzing fear of desolation. Just as Christ's peace works through the agitations rather than despite them, so, too, does this courage work in the midst of fear but without eliminating it. The courage of consolation is an assured confidence that God will provide for those who are doing God's work.

This is the peace, tranquility, and courage of consolation. It is an assurance and confidence in God in the midst of trials, limitations, past failures, and future dangers.

True Perspective: A Subcategory

Just as confusion could be called a subcategory of the disquiet of desolation, so could true perspective be a subcategory of peace and tranquility. A person experiencing consolation is well aware that she does not have all the answers. During early stages of discernment, she may not have any answers at all. But a consoled person does not sweat the problem, because she understands that this is a normal part of human experience and a healthy, perhaps even necessary, stage in good discernment. She is confused about the situation, but she keeps it in perspective. She remembers that she doesn't have to have the answers, because the One who is all-knowing is also all-powerful and all-good. She trusts that God will enlighten her mind when the time is right.

> Not all those who wander are lost.
>
> —J. R. R. Tolkien

In his book *The Holy Longing*, Ronald Rolheiser speaks eloquently about our human frustration with phases of uncertainty and confusion. He says that every worthy Christian endeavor will have its moments of sweating blood in the garden. The mistake would be to allow that confusion and tension to drive us to a hasty reaction that will relieve the tension but not necessarily be a response to God's calling. In consolation, a person can keep the uncertainty, the tension, and the confusion in perspective, trusting that God will act according to the divine timetable.

Great Desires

I call consolation . . . all interior joy that invites and attracts to what is heavenly.

—SE, Rules for Discernment, First Week, #3

Great desires are so much a part of Ignatian spirituality that they call for a more thorough treatment than the other characteristics of consolation. Therefore, much more will be said about these desires in a section of chapter 7 called "Dream the Dreams." For now, we can say that a sure sign of the presence of the true spirit are the holy desires that inflame my heart to do good in the world. In Genesis 1, the reader can sense God's own divine desire to create. One can feel the passion of God the Father who says, "Let there be light" and "Let us make humankind in our image." When I am in tune with God's ever-creative love, I, too, have that passion to create, that desire to bring forth new life. It is one of the holiest aspects of being human.

Transparency

We have already seen how the false spirit works through secrecy. The opposite can be said of the true spirit. "God is light and in him there is no darkness at all," says the first letter of John (1 John 1:5). There is no greater feeling than to bring some dark, private thought into the light. Sharing with a trusted loved one that which has been "kept in the dark" is a liberating experience. Years of high school ministry have taught me that teenagers often make the mistake of thinking that they have to suffer through their growing pains all by themselves—that no one will understand what they are going through. Being a priest, bound by the strict confidentiality of the confessional, I've often had the privilege of being the only one a teenager would truly spill his guts to. When he finally says aloud what has been festering for weeks, months, or sometimes years, I can visibly see the relief in his face and the lightness in his shoulders.

We hope that once a mature Christian has grown out of adolescent fears, she will gather the courage to speak aloud the darker movements inside her *before* they lead to action. Recently I said to my mentor, "I need to tell you about something, not because I think it is a problem but for the sake of transparency." I then told him of feelings I was having that were embarrassing to me—that I would rather not have told anyone. He listened well, and we then had a great conversation about it. Looking back on that moment, I still don't believe the feelings I was having would have become a problem, but I have a strong sense that speaking it aloud to someone provided a fortification against the "agitations and temptations" of the false spirit.

At this point, it might be helpful to look at the characteristics of consolation and desolation, side by side.

Figure 1: Desolation and Consolation, Side by Side	
I am in desolation when I am empty of • Faith, hope, and love • The sense of God's closeness **and full of some combination of** • Disquietude and agitation • Boredom and tepidity • Fear and worry • Secrecy	**I am in consolation when I have** • Faith, hope, and love • The sense of God's closeness • Peace and Tranquility • Great desires • Transparency

Prayer Exercise A: The True Spirit in My Life

1. Begin your prayer time by placing yourself in an alert but comfortable position. Spend a good while quieting yourself and asking the Spirit of God to be present to you and to fill you with life. Soak in the Spirit as you would soak in a warm bath.

2. If you feel called to do so, begin to reflect on a time when you were clearly in a period of consolation—that is, a time of deep inner peace, during which you experienced great desires of faith, hope, and love. It might be a time of exterior sadness or tragedy but of interior peace and tranquility. Ask God to reveal this time to you so that you can learn from it. Go back to that place of deep inner peace. Here are a few ways you might reflect on moments of consolation.

    • Read and ponder the words of Jesus in John 14:27. What is the peace of Christ like? How do you experience it? How is it not the peace that the world gives? Note how this peace does not imply that all interior and exterior problems in your life are solved and resolved but that you have a new and different relationship with those problems.

- Looking back on that period of consolation, ponder how close you felt to God then and how natural it seemed to move toward greater faith, greater hope, and greater love.

- Looking back on that period of consolation, remember how easy it was to recognize "God laboring through all created things and events," as St. Ignatius put it. See how clear it was for you to see God's hand in every aspect of life, even the difficult ones.

PART 2

Responding to Desolation and Consolation

Part 1 introduced the life of St. Ignatius of Loyola and recounted how he got started on his lifelong exploration of the discernment of spirits (chapter 1). Then we looked at a description of the characteristics of the false spirit and its accompanying desolation, and of the true spirit and its accompanying consolation (chapters 2 and 3).

Part 2 presents Ignatius's advice on what to do with this recognition of the true and false spirits. On a daily basis, how are we to feel, think, and act when in desolation? Or when in consolation?

4

When in Desolation

I remember as a boy walking past the fire extinguisher built into the wall at school and reading the large red letters painted on the glass panel: In Case of Fire Break Glass. Being a well-behaved boy in a strict Catholic grade school, I had trouble imagining breaking that glass even if there were a fire. It would certainly have to be a big one in order to explain to the nuns why there was shattered glass on the floor!

One purpose for studying the Ignatian Rules for Discernment is to have at our disposal a means of putting out the fires of desolation. As anyone who has experienced desolation already knows, it is often impossible to eliminate it entirely or immediately. But St. Ignatius teaches that there's much we can do to contain the fire during a period of desolation. This is not lost time, nor is it a time to become passive. It's the time to break the glass! Still, we *must act carefully when in desolation*, says St. Ignatius. This is a tricky time, when it's easy to make mistakes. For that reason, this chapter of the book may be the most important. Following are eight helpful responses to desolation.

Response 1:
Name the Desolation

In the creation story of Genesis 2, God grants Adam the role of naming all the creatures of the earth. This detail isn't meant to be quaint or sentimental; to name something is to have authority over it. When a child names her pet or a sailor names his ship, a relationship is formed, and the one who does the naming has the authority over what has been named. We see this reality not only in Genesis but throughout the Gospels.

- Elizabeth and Zacharias, at the urging of God, are assertive in naming their child John. (Luke 1:5–25, 57–66)
- Jesus makes Simon his own by declaring to him, "I tell you, you are Peter, and on this rock I will build my church." (Matthew 16:13–20)
- In order to expel it, Jesus demands of the unclean spirit, "What is your name?" Likewise, Jesus does not let any unclean spirit name him. (Mark 1:23–28; 1:34; 5:1–10)

In psychology, too, we learn that giving a name to an experience can liberate us. Experiences that go unnamed, however, can frighten or even paralyze us. Psychologist Katherine Clarke defines trauma as "experience seeking articulation." By that she means that we experience trauma when something happens to us that we cannot make sense of. It does not fit our categories. For example, a person who is betrayed by her best friend experiences trauma because this new occurrence (of betrayal) does not fit with the name she has given this person (best friend). The purpose of the therapeutic process, then, is to help the client articulate the experience— to find a way to properly name what has happened. Once a person has successfully done so, the experience may still be painful, but it will no longer be traumatic.

So out of the ground the LORD God formed every animal of the field and every bird of the air, and brought them to the man to see what he would call them; and whatever the man called every living creature, that was its name.
—GENESIS 2:19

The wisdom of Alcoholics Anonymous teaches that the alcoholic's first step of recovery is to name and claim the problem—to say, "My name is Edward, and I am an alcoholic." His alcoholism has been a reality for a long time, but his fear of it kept him from naming it so. Only after naming it aloud can he begin to recover his life.

Consider what often happens during the sacrament of reconciliation. The penitent is burdened by something he's done but has kept it a secret, hidden often away from even his own thoughts. In the confessional, he uses vague terms such as "impure thoughts and actions" to mean masturbation or "irreverence" to mean, "I'm angry with God." The powerful effects of shame make the person afraid to identify the act aloud. I often challenge the penitent to say exactly what he has done. Naming the act in blunt and unambiguous terms reveals its smallness before the mighty love and mercy of God. After doing so, the penitent is visibly relieved. Leaving the act unnamed feeds its power, but naming it allows the person to take ownership of it. Only after he claims the act as his own, can he give it over to Christ.

"Sir?" said Harry. "I've been thinking . . . Sir—even if the Stone's gone, Vol— I mean, You-Know-Who—"

"Call him Voldemort, Harry. Always use the proper name for things. Fear of a name increases fear of the thing itself."
—J. K. ROWLING, HARRY POTTER AND THE SORCERER'S STONE, P. 298

We see that this reality is well established in human experience—in everything from Scripture to Alcoholics Anonymous to the sacraments to pop culture. But how might this insight help us deal with desolation? Consider this story of the person called Noah.

Noah's Story

As prescribed by St. Ignatius, every Jesuit regularly makes the Spiritual Exercises, spending multiple days in silence and prayer, and meeting one-on-one with a retreat director once a day. Noah was a passionate young Jesuit whose retreat was going wonderfully when suddenly one day, out of the blue, he hit a wall.

We had reached the phase of the retreat known as the Third Week, which occurs, as one might expect, around day 21. Ignatius asks the retreatant at this point to accompany Jesus in his passion, to be at his side as he is harassed, arrested, tortured, and killed. Third Week, then, is an example of a time when bad feelings (for example, grief, sorrow, pain) might actually be signs of consolation, because this time of walking with Jesus can lead to more love, faith, and hope.

Thus far, Noah's retreat had been an incredibly joyous experience. Even through the early parts of the retreat, when the person is challenged to look at painful aspects of his life, Noah found the retreat to be freeing and exhilarating. But on this day during the Third Week, Noah came into the office and immediately broke down in tears. He started off our conversation begging me to allow him to do more fasting. It was clear to me that some enormous shift had occurred in him, so I asked him to tell me about his experiences of the day. Frequently interrupted by heartbreaking sobs (up to that point, I'd hardly ever seen him cry), Noah spoke about his experience of accompanying Jesus through his passion. He talked about the pain and fear he saw in Jesus' eyes and how it was more than he could bear. He spoke of the dread of violence in Jesus' voice and how frightened Jesus seemed to be.

As his director, I listened carefully and quietly, encouraging him to describe his experience in more detail. I knew that bad feelings are often a good sign at this point in the retreat, so I thought that

Noah's distress might be a great moment of growth for him. And yet there was something not quite right about the experience. In fact, there were two telltale signs of desolation. First, he was unusually preoccupied with the details of fasting and a fear that he might be doing it wrong (confusion and fear). Second, all through his conversation with me, he kept trying to end it and leave the room (lack of transparency). This was very unusual for Noah, since he normally loved to talk and looked forward to our daily meetings. I had to keep him from leaving several times. Finally, because he couldn't keep still and because I needed to hear more from him, I said, "Let's go for a walk."

On our walk, Noah continued to describe his distressing and disturbing feelings. At one point, I said, "It almost sounds as if what you're describing is despair. Is that right, Noah?"

"Yes! That's exactly what I'm feeling."

"Well, then, I think we have our answer. This experience is not from the true spirit. Despair is the opposite of hope and is practically never a characteristic of the true spirit. Even when a person is feeling unpleasant and uncomfortable feelings, consolation always leads to greater faith, hope, and love. This lack of hope tells us that you are in desolation."

A huge change came over Noah. He said, "Yes, that's it!" and immediately felt relief. It was as though someone had removed an anvil from his back. He suddenly walked lighter and spoke with the contented voice I had grown used to hearing from him. Knowing then that Noah had been experiencing desolation, we could apply some of the insights of Ignatius and move forward fairly easily. The rest of Noah's Third Week was enriching and inspiring.

The moment Noah and I were able to name the experience "desolation," Noah felt instant relief and freedom from it. Those in the presence of the false spirit must follow Jesus' lead in speaking aloud its proper name. To do so will remove a great deal of the power it has taken from us. Recall the story of my anger on the bus trip to Missouri. I experienced a momentary desolation when I struggled to rid myself of this unnamed spirit of anger. As soon as I named and addressed the false spirit, it no longer had power over me. True, it didn't leave me at that time, but it no longer caused disquiet in me—it no longer drove the bus—and therefore was no longer a source of desolation.

Sometimes the "unnamedness" of the experience is the *only* part of it causing desolation. I once worked with a seminarian who throughout his time in the seminary struggled with depression. After months of prayer, therapy, and soul-searching, he finally had the courage to say out loud: "I don't think I really want to be a priest." It was a reality that had struggled to be expressed for a long time, but subconsciously the man thought this truth too frightening to name aloud. Once he could speak it, the work of discernment could truly begin.

These examples reveal how a person might name spiritual desolation in her *prayer* life, but how does this practice of naming desolation work in *everyday* life, outside of prayer time? Often, in the ordinary moments of my day, I act in a way that is inconsistent with my true self. I say something inappropriate; I ignore someone who is trying to reach out to me; I overreact; I gossip; I avoid important work; I yell at the cat. If I stopped and reflected on it a moment, I'd probably say to myself, "Wait a minute. This is not me. What is going on here?" If I scratch beneath the surface, I may discover some desolation lurking beneath. It could be psychological, emotional, or spiritual desolation, or more likely some combination of those. Simply naming the desolating factors beneath my exterior attitudes and actions can go a long way toward moving out of the desolation. If it does not disappear altogether at the moment I name it, then at least I can keep a leash on it. That is, I can choose not to act on those negative emotions. Instead of yelling at the cat, I can stop, take a breath, admit to what I'm actually upset about, and spare the poor cat the onslaught of my wrath.

Response 2:
Avoid Making Changes
or Important Decisions

In a time of desolation we should never make any change, but remain firm and constant in the resolution and decision which guided us the day before the desolation, or in the decision to which we adhered in the preceding consolation. For just as in consolation the good spirit guides and counsels us, so in desolation the evil spirit guides and counsels. Following his counsels we can never find the way to a right decision.

—SE, Rules for Discernment of Spirits, First Week, #5

Rule #5 of St. Ignatius is easy to understand but difficult to apply. Whether desolation has been named or not, it generally makes a good, prayerful Christian very uncomfortable. Often the person will do something—anything—to get out of this discomfort. She may incorrectly conclude that some previous decision was wrong and so attempt to reverse that decision. Or she may think that she must do something different in order to get out of the funk. The problem is that a person loses objectivity when in desolation. Agitation, fear, and confusion lead the person to focus on changes that are at best unnecessary and at worst disastrous. Consider the story of Noah. The first telltale sign of desolation was his very strange distress about the way we had earlier agreed to fast. The two of us had previously decided, *during a time of consolation*, that it would not be good for him to have a traditional fast (that is, abstinence from food). We chose another way that he could make a spiritual sacrifice. Now, in distress, Noah was saying that he "must" fast and that it would be impossible for him to be faithful to the suffering Christ otherwise. Why such a strange fixation on fasting? It is because the desolation had caused him to lose objectivity and to allow less significant concerns to distract him from the love of Christ, which is ultimately the objective of every prayer time.

Theresa's Story

Theresa was a smart, prayerful eighteen-year-old who carefully considered the spiritual implications of her choice of a college. Though she sometimes struggled with low self-esteem, she worked diligently in her classes and managed to graduate near the top of her class. She had many offers from great universities, and her friends and mentors were impressed with her decision-making process. Her father, too, was proud of her and fully supported her decision to go to a Jesuit school on the West Coast. She could tell, though, that he was a little depressed about it, and she suspected it was because the university she chose was across the country from where they lived. Her mother had passed away only a few years before, and the two of them had become closer ever since.

The time came for her to move into the freshman dorm a thousand miles away. In those early days she had a rough time of it. From the very start, she and her roommate did not get along. It was awkward for her to hang out in their dorm room. She also had trouble making friends on campus and often found herself going for long walks alone, thinking of home. When she called her father, he told her how proud he was of her and happy that she was doing so well in her classes. But she was sure she could hear sadness and loneliness in his voice.

Finally, after eight weeks of feeling utterly alone, she met a boy who seemed to like her very much. They went out on several dates, and she was just beginning to feel a little less lonely when suddenly he stopped calling her and would avoid her when she reached out to him. She tried to get him to tell her what was wrong, but this seemed to make him grow more distant.

Meanwhile, her once rich and nourishing prayer life became dry and burdensome. At home, she had grown accustomed to waking up early and praying in her room, but she found this impossible in her awkward dorm-room situation. She prayed in the campus chapel, but she sensed nothing from God. Her prayer felt dry, and she felt restless. She began skipping it altogether.

Everything seemed to be going wrong. True, she was very successful in her classes and enjoyed them. But all the while she kept wondering if she could really make it all the way through law school. Everyone else in her prelaw class had gone to "good" high schools. She feared that her small-town high school education would not get her through the higher-level courses.

One day, after getting no reply from texts she sent to her boyfriend, she went online and bought a plane ticket home. She booked a red-eye flight for late the next day in order to give her time to pack all her stuff and withdraw from the school. When her roommate asked why she was leaving, she snapped at her, saying, "My father needs me, but what do you care?"

This heartbreaking story exemplifies the wisdom of Ignatius's advice not to make a change when in desolation. We can clearly see the signs of desolation:

- Teresa withdraws from school without ever telling anyone of her plans, least of all her father (secrecy).
- She seems to be drifting away from faith, hope, and love by skipping her prayer times (faith), giving up on college (hope), and snapping at her roommate (love).

- Despite the fact that she continues to thrive in her studies, she becomes convinced that she won't succeed in the future (irrational fear of the future, confusion).

From our objective standpoint, we can see how this emotional and spiritual desolation is leading her to draw incorrect conclusions about her present and future life. It is clear for you, the reader, to see this because you have the privilege of standing above the story and looking at it with objectivity. But for anyone going through desolation, the big picture is blurred and obscure. Sadness, fear, boredom, or confusion begins to wear on the desolate person, and she begins to reason poorly. Conclusions she never would come to during a state of consolation suddenly appear to be the best—perhaps even the only—option.

If in those desolate moments of my life I can succeed in the first directive, to name it as desolation, then my next conclusion should be to *draw no more conclusions* without careful consideration and counsel from those who have an objective point of view. This brings us to the third response to desolation.

Response 3:
Rely on Your Support Network

A popular series of cell-phone commercials boasted the strength of network coverage by showing a huge crowd of people following close behind the customer as he walked down the street speaking on his cell phone. That's a good metaphor for the kind of support I'm going to need if I am to live according to God's will. As I make my way through the spiritual life, it is absolutely crucial that I have a strong support network following close behind me, cheering me on, booing the false spirit, whispering tips in my ear, and passing me Gatorade. I will need good mentors, good companions, and a strong link to the church.

Mentors

Years ago, a teenager whose parents were not present in his life said to me, "You know, I just decided that I would have to go out and find my own father figures and mother figures." That was an incredibly wise insight! And it doesn't apply only to people who don't already have strong parental support. There is no reason for me to limit myself to only one mother and one father. After all, even a good mother will be lacking in some areas. Even a good father will have his blind spots.

Support network: Mentors, companions, the church

This idea of going out to find a mentor is one of the best-kept secrets of our time. Perhaps it is the American spirit of independence that doesn't allow me to seek advice from someone wiser than me. Perhaps it is the fast-paced, frenetic world that won't give me the time to consult an elder.

Whatever the reason, I must overcome my reluctance and seek out at least one good and wise mentor in my life. I must commit myself to visiting her regularly. If I don't commit myself, I'll always have excuses for why today is not a good day to pause in my crazy life and go for a visit. If I choose well, my mentor will be perhaps my strongest possible support as I make the day-to-day and the momentous decisions of my life.

What are the qualities of a good mentor?

- A mentor should be wiser (but not necessarily older) than I.
- She should be a very good listener and should neither interrupt nor fade out on me when I am speaking.
- She doesn't necessarily need to be an expert on the particular topic I am discerning, provided she is a good listener and doesn't pretend to be an expert.
- She should have strong self-esteem, such that she doesn't *need* to be my mentor. (If she *needs* to be my mentor, then she will advise me in such a way as to make me dependent on her).
- She should be an affirming presence in my life—she should really believe in me and my ideas.
- However, she should also not be afraid to confront me when she thinks I'm wrong.
- She should never attempt to make a decision for me, even if I am consciously or unconsciously pushing her to do so.
- She should be objective in regard to the decision I am considering. Ideally, then, she should be out of the circle of people who are affected by the decision.
- In other words, she should not be a close member of the family, an immediate superior at work, or a best friend.

Where would I find such a mentor? Chances are, there is already someone in my life who has the qualities of a good mentor and with whom I have enjoyed visiting in the past. Perhaps this person is right under my nose: a neighbor, an aunt, a priest, a coworker. He may not have all the above qualities of an ideal mentor—that's OK. I could settle for someone with most of them. Mentors are people, not heavenly angels.

What should I do once I've found such a person? I take him out to lunch or sit on his porch for a while. I tell him that I am in the process of making an important decision and that I would appreciate it if I could visit with him from time to time. If he agrees and has the time, then I commit myself to coming by at regular intervals, perhaps once a week or once a month.

While my number one mentor is someone who helps me in daily life, I may also want to have secondary mentors with whom I consult about specific areas of my life. Just as I have a general practitioner for general health issues and specialists for particular problems, I may want to have mentors who "specialize." For example, in my own work as a writer, I have a writing mentor with whom I consult before I make important decisions about publishing, signing contracts, and so on. In my early years of teaching high school, I had a mentor teacher for help with problems in the classroom. And I have a formation mentor for the work I do with young Jesuits.

I could have a therapist with whom I consult, especially if there is a lot of emotion around a decision I am currently making. I could also begin to make good use of a too-little-known but priceless gift the church now offers: I could engage in the process of **spiritual direction**.

Going back to the beginning of church history, Christians have sought the wisdom of wise men and women. Over the centuries, this role was often filled by priests and nuns. But now more than ever, the church has many well-trained laywomen and laymen—people in the pews who have families and ordinary jobs—who are accredited spiritual directors. They are trained professionally to listen well to the movements in a person's prayer life and to help her understand what God might be calling her to do or what God is already doing for her.

Spiritual direction: The process of meeting regularly with a person trained to help me with my relationship with God.

How does this process of spiritual direction work? I simply arrange to meet with the director at regular intervals (usually once a month), and I tell her what is going on in my life and in my relationship with God. The director will actively listen and will ask good questions to help me discern God's presence in my life.

How do I find a spiritual director? I could ask around at my local church parish, call the diocese, or search on the Internet. There may also be a nearby retreat house or spirituality center that provides this service. Spiritual Directors International has a directory of certified spiritual directors on their website: www.sdiworld.org.

Companions

We need to draw a distinction between a friend and a **companion**. Let us say that a friend is someone who enjoys my company and whose company I enjoy. I have a good time when he's around. I find myself laughing more, relaxing more. I like his sense of humor and his quirky mannerisms. It is a pleasure to be with him.

Companion: A friend to whom I can entrust the more personal aspects of my life.

But let's say a companion is all this and more. Let's say a companion is someone who deeply desires for me to be my best. A companion is someone who calls forth from me my best self and does so without being bossy, parental, or preachy.

I can name many friends in my life who are fun to be around. I play pool or go to the movies with them. I see them at work or in the neighborhood grocery store. We share a laugh when we're together. Sometimes we have ongoing jokes that last for years. I'm grateful to God for them. But those I name "companion" are on a whole other level. My companions play a pivotal role in my life. We accompany one another on life's most important spiritual journeys. When I'm with my companions, I see more clearly who I am, and I actually like who I am. To borrow a phrase from the movie *As Good as It Gets*, companions make me want to be a better man.

Besides mentors, I need good companions who are no more advanced in the spiritual life than I, who aren't experts in the field of anything I'm discerning, but who sincerely care for me and are willing to look out for me. Unlike the friend with whom I share a laugh or a good movie, I look forward to sharing the deeper parts of myself with my companions, and I look forward to hearing what's going on in the depths of their lives as well.

The Church

When I am in desolation, I need the sure footing of the church. It is my place of refuge when I've lost my sense of direction. During desolation, the church provides a voice of reasoned faith through its teaching and a balm of healing through its rituals.

The church's teaching is the repository of *two thousand years of shared reflection on any spiritual problem I might be experiencing*. Its doctrine is the implementation of that sustained reflection. The church is not always correct, of course. Indeed, over the years of his pontificate, Pope John Paul II apologized to the world for more than one hundred misdeeds of the church throughout its history. But considering the

> Without the food and without the light I wither. Without the bread and without the Bible I wander. Without the Sacrament of life and the book of life, I perish.
>
> —THOMAS À KEMPIS

quantity of doctrines the church has promulgated over the millennia, the mistakes are few and far between.

And—whatever the source of my desolation—there is no other institution that has reflected this long on this very problem of mine. I should never pass up the opportunity to tap into such a fathomless well of reflection and experience. When I am in desolation and am seeking wisdom, I can rely on my own *decades* of reflection and prayer alone, or I can also learn from *thousands of years* of prayer, reflection, debate, moral victories, and—yes—moral failures, too. Why on earth would I pass up such a treasury of wisdom? From Augustine, I learn about surrendering to God's will and forsaking my own hedonistic urgings. From Teresa of Ávila I learn the subtleties, complexities, and ecstasies of contemplative prayer. From Benedict, I learn about hospitality, and from John XXIII, the courage to remake myself. From Mary, I learn to trust in providence, and from Maximilian Kolbe, I learn about sacrifice. From Francis of Assisi, I learn about Lady Poverty, and from Francis Xavier, I learn about passion for evangelization. From Thérèse of Lisieux, I learn about humility, and from Veronica, I learn the power of repentance.

The church is the spiritual refuge for battle-weary souls. I attend church to pray with people who have the same great desires and insipid temptations as I. Together as one family, we lift our prayers to the Father, and we beg the Son to come close—to teach us, to heal us, to redeem us, and to befriend us. When I feel lost, confused, and frightened, the ritual of the church nourishes and strengthens me in a place too deep for words. Ritual allows my body to act out what my soul is longing to articulate. When I am spiritually starving, the Body and Blood are the rations that keep me alive another day. When I am drowning, I hold tight to the lifeline of the rosary. When I am blind and deaf, it is the smell of incense that raises my plea to the heavens.

How to Use My Support Network

Recall Ignatius's politically incorrect metaphor of the false spirit being a seducer of a young maiden who should tell her father everything but is convinced by the rogue to keep it to herself (see page 34). While the metaphor is perhaps a bit inappropriate these days, the point Ignatius makes still stands: when I am in desolation, the self-destructive movement within me will tend to sustain itself by convincing me that I should keep these thoughts, emotions, and actions to myself. Otherwise, a wise mentor or companion will quickly see the falsity in the movement and will help me rid myself of its devastating effects. The supports of my mentors, companions, and the church are my metaphorical fire extinguishers; when things flare up, I'll need to break the glass and put them to work!

I came to Mass today
To hide in Latin words
And smell the dust of ritual.
I came for sanctuary
Where the powerful and poor
Together kneel
And unstoppable time
Holds still
Like a snapshot in the eye of God.
I came to a place without lessons,
Where no one is distilling truth
Like Tennessee Whiskey.
I came to float like a flower
In a Japanese pool.
I came
For the veins under my skin
To swell like the virgin in Nazareth
And burst wine.
I came for something
You cannot get over the counter.
I came because justice
Will not happen before cocktails.
I came because my child's cold
Did not gather in her chest
Like a summer storm.
I came
Because in my nightmare chases
I wake to sweat
The moment before capture.
I came
Because I want it to be true
That I will go in peace
When this Mass is ended.

—John Shea

That is why it is so vital to rely on my support network during desolation and why I must go to my network with everything—absolutely everything. I hold nothing back. This transparency is especially crucial in conversations with my mentor, who will help me absorb and interpret the feedback I'm getting from my prayer, from the church, and from my companions. If I think something is not important enough to discuss with my mentor, I tell her anyway and let her decide whether or not we need to discuss it any further. There is nothing to lose by telling the mentor about it and everything to lose by keeping it a secret.

Especially in times when I have an important decision to make, I will rely on those three lifelines. Provided I have chosen well my mentors and companions, and provided I am faithful to the church, I will almost always find in my support network someone to lead the way as I try to follow God's will. If I feel inclined to proceed in a certain way, I can bounce this idea off my mentors and companions and bump it up against the teaching of the church. If I am in sync with God's will, the three supports (or at least two out of three) will almost always align. If one or two of them seem to be on a different page, then I must slow down my discernment and seek greater clarity and consensus. If all three of them are opposed to what I'm proposing to do, then there's a good chance that I'm simply wrong. In all my years as a Christian adult, I can't recall a single moment when all three of my supports were opposed to what was ultimately the right thing to do. While I do not slavishly submit to any one of them, I do take each of them seriously, and I trust their consensus almost as much as I trust my own inclinations. Why? Because, unlike me, these supports will have more objectivity about the matter at hand than I have. I am necessarily emotionally attached to my inclinations, and to that extent, I am vulnerable to irrationality. My emotions, while often helpful, can fog my vision. The objectivity of these supports allows them to see right through the fog—to have a broader and therefore more accurate vision.

Response 4:
Consider Potential Logistical, Moral, or Psychological Problems

Ignatius tells us that God never *causes* desolation. God, however, does *permit* desolation to come. Why? Ignatius has three suppositions:

More will be mentioned of the second two causes of desolation in other parts of the book (see Response 8, page 100). In this section, I would like to address the first cause of desolation. Here is how Ignatius puts it:

> *The first [cause for desolation] is because we have been tepid and sloth-ful or negligent in our exercises of piety, and so through our own fault spiritual consolation has been taken away from us.*
>
> —SE, RULES FOR DISCERNMENT OF SPIRITS, FIRST WEEK, #9

Of the three causes, only this first one implies culpability on my part. It's important to note that if I am in desolation *I should not presume that it is my fault.* On the contrary, for a devout Christian, desolation does *not* usually come because of sin.

Furthermore, even within this first cause, I would like to propose a qualifier to Ignatius's rule. I believe that in addition to moral problems that lead to desolation, there could be logistical problems or psychological problems as well. Ignatius did not include these possibilities because the sixteenth-century mind-set tended to blame "the sinner" for even logistical problems and because the entire field of psychology had not yet come about.

With this in mind, I propose that the first reason desolation has come is because of moral, logistical, or psychological problems. When a person finds himself in desolation, then, it would be good to do a sort of inventory of these three factors to see if, by making some changes here or there, he might begin to ease out of desolation.

Figure 2: Ignatius's Three Causes of Desolation
1. I have fallen into sin and God has allowed desolation to come as a natural consequence.
2. God allows desolation to come in order to "test me." He knows that some gifts and graces come only through struggle on my part. Much like a teacher who tests even her gifted students in order that they grow stronger in the field, so does God allow desolation to challenge and stretch me.
3. God allows desolation to come in order to give me the great gift of humility, which is a core virtue for Ignatius and of which Ignatius says one could never have enough. If my spiritual life were filled with nothing but consolation, I could well become spiritually prideful. I could begin to think that I am the source of the graces that come from God. God allows desolation to remind me that "all is the gift and grace of god our Lord" and that I can do nothing without him.

Moral Problems

Most of the time, desolation will come for reasons other than sin. There are times, however, when desolation is the natural consequence of my own attitudes, actions, or omissions. When I find myself in desolation, I should examine my conscience to explore whether I might have made a poor moral choice somewhere along the way. Have I been unkind to my loved ones? Have I been dishonest in business or in my schoolwork? Have I over-indulged in physical pleasures and instant gratification? Have I neglected my relationship with God? with the church? with my loved ones? with myself? Have I become lazy? prideful? Have I grown materialistic? petty? Am I a gossip? Have I neglected the poor? Have I squandered the earth's resources? Have I failed to keep the Ten Commandments? Have I become overly scrupulous, obsessed with the rules or with always being right?

The fallout of sinful attitudes and actions will reverberate through every aspect of my life, including my prayer life. A more careful reading of Ignatius suggests that sinful *inactions*, what the church calls sins of omission, may be an even more common cause. He suggests that desolation might have come because "we are tepid, slothful, or negligent." Taking his advice, the person in desolation will want to look especially to those particular sins. Have I neglected my prayer? my mission in life? my loved ones? Have I neglected the poor and needy of the world? Is there a painful decision that I am avoiding? From what disturbing reality am I hiding?

Logistical Problems

If sin is not the culprit for desolation, perhaps the problem lies with some logistical detail. I may want to consider with my spiritual director or mentor a simple change in the details concerning my prayer. Often, making a simple adjustment regarding when, where, or how long I pray will do the trick. Here are some questions I could explore:

- **When:** Am I praying at the best time of day? For example, if I leave prayer for the very end of my day, when I am exhausted— if I'm throwing God the scraps of my time and energy—then my prayer life will suffer. Even if I am giving God the best part of my day, I may want to move to some other good time slot just to shake things up a bit. For example, I may move my prayer time from early morning to early evening.
- **Where:** Have I chosen the best place to pray? Are there too many distractions in that location? Or maybe it's too quiet? Is it comfortable enough? Or is it so comfortable that I'm falling

asleep every day? What about my prayer position? Should I try sitting up instead of reclining? Should I pray while walking? Ignatius himself seemed to prefer lying flat on his back—should I try that?

- **How long:** Is my prayer time too long or too short? This is a particularly good question to explore with a spiritual director.

- **With what resources:** Am I choosing good Scripture passages over which to pray? Is there a prayer book that helps me pray when I get stuck? Is there some spiritual reading that I could do to fan the flames? Could I include some object in my prayer, such as a cross, a candle, a rosary, a painting, an icon, a photograph, a leaf, or a rock?

- **With whom:** Do I engage in regular spiritual direction? Is there some prayer group in my local church that I could join? Have I kept up with my spiritual companions? Could I strike up a new spiritual friendship?

- **What prayer style:** Should I try switching the type of prayer that I'm doing? Should I switch from the rosary to meditation and contemplation, for example? Should I try centering prayer, *lectio divina*, the way of the cross, eucharistic adoration, praise and worship, the Liturgy of the Hours, or petitionary prayer? Perhaps I should try some different combination of prayer styles. If I always begin with petitionary prayer and then move to meditation, for example, perhaps I could try switching the order and beginning with meditation.

Sometimes, the problem is not that I am doing something wrong in my prayer but simply that my prayer has gotten a little stale and a change would be refreshing. Just because praying early in the morning has always worked for me in the past, I should not presume that it is the best time slot for me in the present. If meditation and contemplation are the center of my prayer life, perhaps I should grab my rosary and go for a walk for the next few days. I must remember that God is the one who does the heavy lifting in prayer and that God greatly desires for our relationship to deepen. Therefore, any attempt to reach for God will in fact reach God, even if I don't always sense God's presence.

It could be that life circumstances will force me to make changes in the way I pray. I remember one period when I was so incredibly busy from sunup to sundown that no matter what time I sat in my favorite prayer chair, I instantly fell fast asleep. After several failed attempts to stay awake, I reluctantly chose to go for a reflective walk instead. I *reluctantly* did so because normally my prayer tends to be more superficial if I am walking rather than sitting. This switch, however, began a long period of fruitful and grace-filled prayer.

I may want to explore the impact of my life circumstances on daily prayer. Am I getting enough sleep? enough exercise? Is my diet affecting my prayer? Am I too stressed to pray? Am I too inactive? Has fatigue, physical illness, or disability affected my prayer? Has a change in my living situation influenced my spiritual life?

One cautionary note: While I am making adjustments to the way I do prayer, I must keep in mind that Ignatius warned sternly against making big changes while in desolation. It could be a mistake, therefore, to make a big switch in the way I pray. For example, desolation may be coming to me because of the other two causes (testing and humility). If that is the case, it probably would not be a good idea to make any changes in the way I pray. Instead, I should hold on and persevere in my prayer. I should allow God to stretch me or make me humble as I struggle to remain present in desolate prayer.

How then do I decide whether or not to make changes in the logistics of my prayer? It depends on the situation.

- Some of the needs for change will be obvious and simple to discern. If I find myself falling asleep in prayer every day, for example, then I certainly need to change either the way I pray or the way I sleep.
- Some of the changes may be so small that there's no need to worry about trying them. It's hard to imagine that trying out a new small gesture such as lighting a candle or holding a crucifix would cause problems.
- However, if the change that I'm considering isn't so obviously necessary (changing sleep patterns) or innocuous (lighting a candle), then it would be best to discuss the change with my spiritual director or mentor beforehand. The greater the impact of the change, the more cautious I should be to make it.

Psychological Problems

Perhaps the roots of the desolation are psychological rather than spiritual. Ignatian scholar Father Timothy Gallagher emphasizes the need to distinguish spiritual desolation from emotional or psychological desolation. The two are closely related, of course. Spiritual desolation will influence my emotional well-being and vice versa, but nonetheless, it is important to discover: What is the source of the desolation? Where is it rooted?

Mari's Story

Mari had been enjoying a healthy prayer life for three years when she suddenly seemed to slip into desolation. In her prayer time, she felt as though she were a bag of dry bones. The more she called out to God for solace, the emptier and lonelier she felt. She found herself fluctuating between feeling guilty for something she must have done wrong—though she didn't know what—and angry at God for abandoning her.

Meanwhile, outside her prayer life, Mari experienced long bouts of depression. This depression was unusual in that there seemed to be no cause for it. She had a loving husband and beautiful children. As a doctor, Mari had a stable and healthy medical practice. She had no major physical problems.

Mari had never been in the practice of regularly meeting with a spiritual director. But a Christian blog she enjoyed reading greatly extolled the practice of ongoing spiritual direction. During a particularly dry and depressing week, Mari decided to give it a try. She called the local spirituality center in her diocese and began to see Beth, a laywoman trained in the art of direction.

Beth and Mari began to explore the possibilities of what might be causing the desolation. They considered the moral and logistical aspects of Mari's life. Beth suggested books about how one might spiritually grow through periods of dryness. While these explorations helped a little in the short run, they did little to help Mari's long-term emotional and spiritual state.

Beth began to ask more questions about Mari's depression. She, too, could see no exterior factors in Mari's life that might cause depression. Still, she suggested that Mari give psychotherapy a try. Mary was reluctant at first but eventually gathered the courage to call the therapist. After several sessions, Mari found the experience of therapy OK, but she did not seem to be getting any better. The therapist then suggested something that really frightened Mari: perhaps the root cause of her depression was a chemical imbalance. Being a doctor, Mari knew well that, just as some people need to take insulin for diabetes and others have to take cholesterol medication for heart problems, others need medications to balance the biochemistry of the brain. She knew that for some people, depression was largely due not to life circumstances but to medical issues that could be resolved only through medication. She knew all this from her own medical training, but from an emotional standpoint, she had to work through the irrational stigma of taking medication for psychological health.

After several months of taking a mild antidepressant and of regular therapy and spiritual direction, Mari experienced a dramatic though gradual change in her life. Though the therapy and spiritual direction were nurturing and helpful, everyone felt confident that it was the medication that truly made the difference. Mari now felt that she could concentrate again and that she was not preoccupied by irrational and insignificant concerns. This change in her daily life was also present in her prayer life. It became fairly easy again to praise God in the psalms and to hear his voice speaking to her through the Beatitudes. More than anything, Mari experienced healing in her prayer life when she meditated on all that had occurred through the process of psychotherapy. She felt that the therapist and the medication were truly God's instruments of healing her life.

Father William Huete, one of my mentors in formation work, is fond of saying, "We must deal with spiritual problems spiritually and psychological problems psychologically." Good Christians often make the mistake of thinking that there is something wrong with their moral lives when, in reality, the cause of the problem is psychological. If it is a fairly serious psychological problem, it would be impossible to find the solutions to the problem through prayer alone. It would be like consulting the Bible to learn how to make chicken gumbo. God has gifted the world with medical technology and with advances in psychotherapy. God wants us to receive these gifts and to utilize them as we proceed through life and continue to grow spiritually.

Response 5:
Be Aware of the False "Angel of Light"

The fifth response is to more subtle movements of the false spirit. The person must recognize the false "angel of light" in her life. She must notice that some of the urgings and desires that *seem* holy and good on the surface are actually distractions from what she is called to do.

Reviewing the Past

When the enemy of our human nature has been detected and recognized by the trail of evil making his course and by the wicked end to which he leads us, it will be profitable for one who has been tempted to review immediately the whole course of the temptation. Let him consider the series of good thoughts, how they arose, how the evil one gradually attempted to make him step down from the state of spiritual delight and joy in which he was, till finally he drew him to his wicked designs. The purpose of this review is that once such an experience has been understood and carefully observed, we may guard ourselves for the future against the customary deceits of the enemy.

—SE, RULES FOR DISCERNMENT OF SPIRITS, SECOND WEEK, #6

For a devout Christian, desolation often begins with good thoughts, feelings, or actions. As I look back through the history of my descent into desolation, perhaps there were several stages during which the movements seemed holy and good. But at some point things began to feel a little different—something felt not quite right. This is the crucial moment to investigate: What was that not-quite-right feeling like? How did I respond to that feeling? Did I ignore it? overcompensate for it? Was I consciously aware of it, or was it more of an unconscious sense? Did I write about it in

89

my journal? Did I talk about it with anyone? What exactly was the attractive thought, emotion, or action that turned out to be the false spirit in the guise of the angel of light?

Looking back at the story of Noah (see page 65), we see that he began with holy attractions: to fast and to feel sorrow for Jesus' suffering in the passion. Both of these movements can be good and virtuous. But in Noah's case there was something not quite right about them. Looking back on the experience, Noah perhaps might be able to pinpoint the very moment of the shift toward desolation. Perhaps he had not slept enough the night before. Perhaps he was trying too hard to have a good retreat. Perhaps he began to feel pressure to "suffer hard" for Jesus. Perhaps there was some hidden sadness, resentment, anxiety, fear, or confusion that he was not able to admit to himself at the time. Exploring these questions with a good spiritual director would give Noah valuable information about ways in which he is susceptible to being misguided. That knowledge will serve him well in the future; he may be able to recognize the false spirit much earlier next time and therefore will be able to make proactive changes.

Preparing for the Future

If I am currently in a state of desolation, then I am especially vulnerable to deception by the false angel of light. Any time the psyche is uncomfortable with its current state, it will work to flee the discomfort. For the devout Christian, escape from the pain will often be in the form of some "holy" action that is in fact not an appropriate response to the situation.

Consider the case of Theresa, the lonely college student (see page 70). She is in a terribly desolate moment: she feels alone and abandoned, even by God. It is completely natural for her psyche to begin to search for a way out. But because she is a good person who takes her responsibilities seriously, her psyche will not allow her simply to flee, so the spirit of desolation dresses up the notion of leaving in a cloak of holiness: *My father needs me. He sacrificed so much for me when Mom died, now I must sacrifice for him by coming home to him.* How could Theresa tell that these holy notions are from the false spirit? She could observe that they bear the signs of the false spirit:

- They are leading her to make a change during desolation—a change from a good discernment she made back when she was in consolation.
- She is drawn to do this "holy act" without telling anyone about it first. She seems drawn to keep these holy thoughts a secret from everyone, even her father. If these thoughts were truly from the good spirit, there would be no reason to keep them a secret.

What can we learn from Theresa's story? We can learn that, when in desolation, we will be tempted to do things that seem "good and holy" but that do not withstand the Ignatian tests (Am I drawn to make a change while in desolation? Am I drawn to secrecy?). When in desolation, I should look out for and resist any "good" temptations of the false angel of light.

The Old Testament character of Job is rightly considered a hero of desolation. God, in the end, declares that Job has "spoken of me what is right" (Job 42:7) while Job's so-called friends have not spoken correctly. This is astonishing, given that his friends say "holy things" about God's goodness and Job actually rages *against* God. Job's friends are the false angels tempting Job in the midst of his desolation to do incorrect "holy" actions. They want him to confess sins that he hasn't committed and to grovel before God. Job resists the temptation to do what looks holier but is, in fact, dishonest. Instead, he does the unthinkable: He challenges God to a contest of wits. He accuses and scolds God. But God is pleased with Job's honesty and integrity, and he reprimands Job's "holier" friends for their "folly" (Job 42:8).

Theresa's and Job's stories are dramatic, but the temptation to follow the false angel of light occurs in ordinary ways as well. For example, at a time when I should be gentle with myself, I might overwork myself or go overboard in volunteerism. In a moment when I feel disconnected and need to be with people, I might force myself to leave my group of friends because "I don't want to bring them down."

How do I guard against this false angel of light? I do not take any holy attractions at face value. I test them using Ignatius's insights. Will this action lead to greater faith, hope, and love in me? Am I making a crucial change during desolation? Am I transparent with my mentors and companions, or would I hesitate to tell them about this attraction? Am I attracted to this action right now because it would be a means of escaping an uncomfortable situation?

Response 6:
Be Firm with the False Spirit
and Work Diligently

Ignatius wisely advises that we not reverse a decision that was properly discerned while in consolation. He does, however, allow for (and even encourages) another type of change:

> *Though in desolation we must never change our former resolutions, it will be very advantageous to intensify our activity against the desolation.*
>
> —SE, RULES FOR DISCERNMENT OF SPIRITS, FIRST WEEK, #6

I shouldn't change my well-discerned proposals, says Ignatius, but I should change myself in actively working against the spirit of desolation. Unfortunately, the desolation will tempt me to do the opposite: to change my properly made decisions but to remain interiorly passive as disquietude, confusion, anger, and fear get the best of me. It is the loss of hope that leads me unconsciously to surrender to these agitations. Ignatius insists that I fan the flame of hope within myself by aggressively resisting desolation.

Being passive in the face of desolation will only increase its power and control over me. Resisting it will limit its influence. Using a contemporary metaphor, Jesuit father David Fleming loosely translates Ignatius's insight:

> *The evil spirit often behaves like a spoiled child. If a person is firm with children, children give up petulant ways of acting. But if a person shows indulgence or weakness in any way, children are merciless in trying to get what they want, stomping their feet in defiance or wheedling their*

way into favor. So our tactics must include firmness in dealing with the evil spirit in our lives.*

Having worked in high schools for nine years, I can think of a thousand examples of great teachers who use discipline to deal with spoiled children and of weak teachers who fail miserably by attempting to sweet-talk them instead. When in desolation, I must treat the false spirit as a spoiled child. I must firmly insist that its agitations "keep still." This firmness might dispel desolation completely—and it might not. But even if the desolation isn't eliminated, it will not have so strong a hold.

How, in practical ways, do I work against desolation in everyday life?

- In my prayer and in conversations with loved ones, I can name the desolation and its accompanying agitations.
- With the help of a spiritual director or a companion, I can make firm decisions about what I will and will not do in the face of these agitations.
- If I cannot make them go away altogether, I can then draw a line in the sand and tell these spoiled children, "You may go no further." For example, if I am experiencing fear as I prepare for a presentation at work, I can go to prayer and, with Jesus at my side, say, "I may not be able to get rid of my fear, but I will not let it keep me from succeeding in the presentation. Fear might remain with me, but it cannot and will not drive my actions."
- If I'm in a dark mood of bitterness, I can choose not to allow this darkness to spread to my actions toward others. Instead, I can make a choice to be *extra* kind and gentle to the people I meet, despite desolation's urgings that I sneer at them.

---

*David A. Fleming, *Draw Me into Your Friendship: The Spiritual Exercises: A Literal Translation & a Contemporary Reading* (St. Louis: The Institute of Jesuit Sources, 1996), 257.

- If I feel inclined to stay in my room and sulk all day, I will choose the opposite path by stepping out of the house and socializing with people. This Ignatian practice of doing the opposite, or of consciously overcompensating, is sometimes referred to as the practice of **agere contra**, literally, to "act against."

Agere contra: Literally, to "act against," the choice to do the opposite of what I am tempted to do in desolation.

Increase Prayer and Church Activity

In two different sections of Ignatius's *Spiritual Exercises*, he recommends that we "act against" desolation by increasing prayer and church participation:

> We must remember that during the time of consolation it is easy, and requires only a slight effort, to continue a whole hour in contemplation, but in time of desolation it is very difficult to do so. Hence, in order to fight against the desolation and conquer the temptation, the exercitant must always remain in the exercise a little more than the full hour. Thus he will accustom himself not only to resist the enemy, but even to overthrow him.
>
> —SE, ANNOTATION 13

And in another place:

> Though in desolation we must never change our former resolutions, it will be very advantageous to intensify our activity against the desolation. We can insist more upon prayer, upon meditation, and on much examination of ourselves. We can make an effort in a suitable way to do some penance.
>
> —SE, RULES FOR DISCERNMENT OF SPIRITS, FIRST WEEK, #6

Because feeling distant from God is one of the central characteristics of desolation, prayer can be an arduous task. Like our unfortunate college friend Theresa, many people in desolation either stop praying altogether or begin to skim a little off the top. If my daily practice is to pray for thirty minutes, for example, I may find myself leaving prayer after twenty or twenty-five minutes. It's not hard to imagine the following week slipping further down the slope to ten or fifteen minutes, and so on. During desolation, I may need to make a firm commitment to prayer. As recommended by Ignatius, I might want to make a symbolic gesture of resistance to the desolation by *adding* a few minutes to the end of it. If I find myself constantly looking at my watch during prayer, I might set the alarm for the designated time and put the watch out of reach.

I also might find it difficult to attend church during desolation. I may unconsciously seek excuses to show up late or to leave early. In the spirit of *agere contra*, I may want to commit myself to attend church one more time per week than I normally do.

If I am in the regular practice of spiritual direction, it is imperative that I not cancel any meetings. If the desolation is particularly intense, the director may even recommend that I come at a greater frequency for a while.

One caution: in the effort to practice *agere contra* in prayer and church life, we will again have to beware of the false angel of light. Often a very religious person who is bored or restless in prayer will punish himself unconsciously for his "bad behavior" of being bored by forcing himself to pray an inordinate amount of time. Notice in Ignatius's instructions that he recommends only that the person pray "somewhat more" than the accustomed time as opposed to something radical like doubling the time. A radical increase will only cause spiritual burnout and further grief. Any major shifts in prayer during desolation, then, should be discussed first with a mentor or spiritual director.

Response 7:
Be Gentle, Patient, and Encouraging
to Yourself

While Ignatius would have the person in desolation be firm and disciplined toward the false spirit, he would recommend that she be gentle, patient, and encouraging to herself during this difficult time:

> When one is in desolation, he should strive to persevere in patience. This reacts against the vexations that have overtaken him.
>
> —*SE*, RULES FOR DISCERNMENT OF SPIRITS, FIRST WEEK, #7

St. Ignatius is not often praised for his gentleness. This retired Basque soldier of the fifteenth century had a past that was rough around the edges, to say the least. He often used military metaphors for his relationship with Christ and for his Christian endeavors. He was known as being a difficult man to work for: demanding, serious, and quick to give criticism. It is all the more striking, then, how tenderly he treated those struggling with desolation. If a director sees that the directee is in desolation, Ignatius advises, "let him not deal severely and harshly with him, but gently and kindly. He should encourage and strengthen him for the future" (*SE*, Annotation 7). He knows from personal experience that the "vexations which come to him" lead the desolate person to be impatient with himself, to judge himself harshly. Therefore, to act against (*agere contra*) the inclinations of the false spirit is to work at being gentle with oneself.

Recall Marty's experience (p.46), which we spoke of earlier:

> When he approached the moment of praying over Christ's passion, he felt nothing at all at first. Then he felt frustration at his inability to feel anything as he watched Christ suffer for him. As the retreat

went on, the frustration turned to self-loathing, so much so that by the end of this phase of the retreat, Marty was no longer focused on Jesus at all but rather on his own seemingly cold heart.

As hard as Ignatius could be on himself and on his assistants, he insisted on gentleness with those in desolation because the harsh self-treatment of the desolate person does not lead to greater faith, hope, and love. As we can see in Marty's story, it does not lead the person to focus on Christ's love and mercy but rather on his own wretchedness.

Because hope, in particular, suffers during desolation, Ignatius encourages the director to give the desolate person "courage and strength (Annotation 7)." As Ignatian scholar Timothy Gallagher so beautifully points out, Ignatius encourages the desolate person to trust that Christ "has left him in trial in his natural powers, so that he may resist . . . since *he can resist* with the divine help, which always remains with him, though he does not clearly feel it." *He can resist*, insists Ignatius. "Let the one who is in desolation think that he can do much."*

> When one is in desolation, he should be mindful that God has left him to his natural powers to resist the different agitations and temptations of the enemy in order to try him. He can resist with the help of God, which always remains, though he may not clearly perceive it. For though God has taken from him the abundance of fervor and overflowing love and the intensity of His favors, nevertheless, he has sufficient grace for eternal salvation.
>
> —SE, RULES FOR DISCERNMENT OF SPIRITS, FIRST WEEK, #7

---

*Timothy Gallagher, *The Discernment of Spirits* (New York: Crossroad, 2005), 100–101.

How—in concrete, specific action—do I practice gentleness, patience, and encouragement with myself during desolation?

- First, since the desolation inclines me to judge myself harshly, I practice *agere contra* by speaking kindly to myself. "I'm doing OK . . . I'm going to get through this . . . It isn't as bad as it feels right now . . . God loves me and I love myself." I say the things a good mother would say to a wounded child.

- Second, I remind myself that desolation rarely lasts for very long. "Let him think that he will soon be consoled," says Ignatius. Holding on to that hope will help move the process along. Even Job, the icon of the faithful desolate man, spent less than 1 percent of his entire life in desolation. The rest of his life, both before and after the desolation, was joyous and enriching.

- Third, except through my prayer life and positive attitude, desolation is normally *not* the time for bold moves. Instead, if possible, I sit quietly and patiently, actively waiting for God to make the next move, and believing that he will. My own novice master once said, "If you're traveling on a horse through the desert and a sandstorm kicks up, get off your horse, lie face down on the ground, and wait it out." If at all possible, I lie low for a while and try to enjoy this low-profile life.

- Fourth and finally, I remind myself that God is all-loving and all-powerful and will not send me any challenges I can't handle. If that is true, then I can live through this challenge, and I'll even trust that God will make *good use* of it, which brings us to the last response I should make to my experience of desolation.

Response 8:
Have Faith That God Will Make Good Use of This Desolation

Ignatius was far more concerned with the person who experienced neither consolation nor desolation—the person who seemed to be tone deaf to the spirits—than he was with the person in desolation. He instructs the retreat director to be very concerned about and to investigate thoroughly the cases in which "no spiritual movements, such as consolations or desolations, come to the soul of him who is exercising himself, and that he is not moved by different spirits." For this person, the director must "inquire carefully of him" about the concrete experience of prayer, looking for what might be going wrong (*SE*, Annotation 6, trans. Fleming). This situation of "no spiritual movements" is the one in which little growth can take place.

Desolation, however, is not a wasted period. It's an opportunity to receive the more difficult graces that can come only through a bit of suffering. Remember that, while God never brings desolation, God does allow it and would never do so unless we could grow from the experience. It was through the experience of crying out to God that Job encountered God in a transcendent way. And through this experience of desolation and redemption, Job became far more blessed (wiser, holier, more successful) than before the desolation. Like Job, I can look back at the darkest times of my life and see that it was in those times that I grew the most.

Ignatius suggests three difficult graces in particular that the desolate one has the potential of receiving: repentance, fortitude, and humility. I would suggest others as well: patience, trust, self-assurance, self-confidence, wisdom, and unwavering loyalty toward God and toward Christian commitments. Christianity's central story of resurrection through the cross of Christ is the testimony that God can transform even evil occurrences into the means of salvation. These dark times can be breakthrough moments in our own salvation history.

In part 3, we will learn how a person can use desolation almost as much as consolation when discerning a big decision. We can use desolation as a sort of negative indicator of God's will. For example, the discerner could pray over various options, imagining himself having lived with option A, then with option B, and so on. If he experiences desolate movements (fear; tepidity; a lack of faith, hope, and love) when imagining one particular option, it could be a sign that this option is not God's will.

What Captain Steve Taught Me

One day my brother Steve took me sailing on his little sunfish sailboat. I never really got the hang of running, reaching, jibing and tacking, but I did enjoy watching in fascination as Steve expertly took us in any direction to which I pointed. Embarrassingly asking about how will we return home unless the wind changes direction, I learned that a good sailor can use practically any wind to go in whatever direction he desires. This was a huge revelation for me! I naively thought that one would have to travel in the direction of the wind at all times. Sailing, I discovered, is about detecting the source of the wind, then making adjustments to harness that wind to move the boat forward. This is a perfect analogy for using discernment of spirits to progress in the spiritual life. We pay attention to learn the source of this particular movement, then we make spiritual adjustments to harness this movement (whether it be consolation or desolation) in order to move forward in the spiritual life. It is only when there is no wind at all that we cannot move forward. I do not fear desolation then; I welcome it and utilize it for God's greater glory. It's the ultimate practical joke that God and I play on the false spirit.

In Case of Fire . . .

If the desolate person breaks the glass on the fire-extinguisher case by naming aloud the desolation and then by actively working against it, desolation could at worst have minimal negative consequences and at best be a moment of grace. Looking back on three of our stories, we can see how the above eight responses to desolation can aid the desolate one and help turn this difficult moment into one of grace:

- Noah was courageous enough *not* to make a change in his fasting before consulting his support network. Together, after recognizing and naming the false spirit in what looked like the angel of light, we chose to work firmly against this movement and to adjust his prayer life gently. Noah now looks at that moment in the retreat as a crucial one when he grew tremendously.

- Had Theresa chosen not to make a decision during desolation but instead to speak to her father, she would not have left school so abruptly. He would have helped Theresa name this urge to go home as a false angel of light, providing her an escape from the pain of loneliness and hurt. Together they could have explored the logistical problems (such as her poor living situation) and made proactive choices to make her daily life a little more pleasant. More than anything, her father could have spoken sweetly to her and encouraged her, telling her that she was in the right place and that she was too smart and talented to drop out of school.

- Mari was mature enough to remain faithful to her prayer despite its dryness and to consult mentors and experts in spirituality, psychology, and medicine. In doing so, she discovered that her desolation was more of a psychological nature rather than a spiritual one. She kept her hope alive by not giving up as she moved from spirituality to psychotherapy to medication. She patiently tried a variety of solutions and eventually found the help she needed.

A person must respond to hazardous situations with precision and single-mindedness; he or she must know well what to do and what not to do. If the fire of desolation ignites in my spiritual life, I must know the right and wrong ways of dealing with it. Responding properly will not only avert disaster; it may well lead to abundant grace.

Figure 3: Eight Ways to Deal with Desolation
1. Name it.
2. Make no unnecessary changes.
3. Rely on your support network.
4. Consider logistical or moral causes.
5. Be aware of the false angel of light.
6. Be firm with the false spirit.
7. Be gentle with yourself.
8. Have faith that God is at work in your desolation.

I shall die, but
That is all that I shall do for Death.
I hear him leading his horse out of the
    stall;
I hear the clatter on the barn-floor.
He is in haste; he has business in Cuba,
Business in the Balkans, many calls to
    make this morning.
But I will not hold the bridle
While he clinches the girth.
And he may mount by himself:
I will not give him a leg up.

Though he flick my shoulders with his
    whip,
I will not tell him which way the fox
    ran.
With his hoof on my breast, I will not
    tell him where

The black boy hides in the swamp.
I shall die, but that is all that I shall do
    for Death;
I am not on his pay-roll.

I will not tell him the whereabouts of
    my friends
Nor of my enemies either.
Though he promise me much,
I will not map him the route to any
    man's door.
Am I a spy in the land of the living,
That I should deliver men to Death?
Brother, the password and the plans of
    our city
Are safe with me; never through me
Shall you be overcome.

—EDNA ST. VINCENT MILLAY

5

When in Consolation

I call it consolation when an interior movement is aroused in the soul, by which it is inflamed with love of its Creator and Lord, and as a consequence, can love no creature on the face of the earth for its own sake, but only in the Creator of them all. It is likewise consolation when one sheds tears that move to the love of God, whether it be because of sorrow for sins, or because of the sufferings of Christ our Lord, or for any other reason that is immediately directed to the praise and service of God. Finally, I call consolation every increase of faith, hope, and love, and all interior joy that invites and attracts to what is heavenly and to the salvation of one's soul by filling it with peace and quiet in its Creator and Lord.

—*SE*, Rules for Discernment of Spirits, First Week, #3

In souls that are progressing to greater perfection, the action of the good angel is delicate, gentle, delightful. It may be compared to a drop of water penetrating a sponge.

—Rules, Second Week, #7

Asking what to do when in consolation is like going to my doctor to ask if there is anything I should do about all this good health I've been having lately. I presume the doctor would say, "Go live!" And so it is with consolation. My chief task is to go live! To go do something beautiful with my life. To do what humans were created to do, which for Ignatius meant "praise, reverence, and serve God our Lord." This is my ultimate purpose, or as Ignatius put it, my "First Principle and Foundation." It is the topic of part 3, the final part of this book.

But healthy people do, in fact, go to see their doctors. They go for a checkup, which involves various tests to determine if there are unseen problems and also to prevent potential problems from ever existing. And so, aside from my chief task of living out my First Principle and Foundation, I should do regular checkups when in consolation to discern underlying spiritual problems or to prevent potential problems from occurring. Ignatius put it this way:

> *When one enjoys consolation, let him consider how he will conduct himself during the time of ensuing desolation, and store up a supply of strength as defense against that day.*
>
> —SE, RULES FOR DISCERNMENT OF SPIRITS, FIRST WEEK, #10

But why on earth would I want to return to the problems of my last desolation once it is over? Why not simply be grateful that I am out of desolation now and move forward rather than look back?

As a pastoral counselor for adolescents, I found it frustrating that teenagers often waited until it was too late to seek pastoral or emotional help. By the time they came to see me, the problem had already spun out of control, and there was little we could do about it. I remember getting a phone call from one of my students, with whom I'd had a good counseling relationship. He told me that he had been caught with marijuana on the campus and was told that he would have to withdraw from the school. He asked if there was anything I could do. I thought, *Well, friend, there was much that I could have done had you told me you had this problem before you got caught. But now, it is too late. We cannot uncrack an egg.*

I also remember several cases in which a teenager would want to speak with me when at the lowest point of depression, rage, anxiety, or fear. I would do my best to help him hold on through the tempest. But once the moment had passed, I never saw him again until he was back at that lowest point. Each time he pulled out of the dark moment, he would prefer to carry on as if nothing had happened. He never gave me the opportunity to work with him in the clear light of day.

If my dad and I are fishing and we discover a hole in the bottom of the boat, we would be foolish to try to make a perma-

> Run while you have the light of life.
> —RULE OF BENEDICT

nent repair while out on the water, far from shore. Our objectives at the moment are clear: plug the hole as well as possible and start bailing as we race back to land! Only when we make it back will we be able to lift the boat out of the water and make the repair on the *underside* of the boat. In the same way, I can't make lasting changes while in the midst of desolation. My objectives at that moment are clear: plug the hole, bail, and get back to land! Only when I am on the sure footing of consolation will I be able to work on the problem below the surface.

Why is consolation, as opposed to desolation, the right time to work on the problem? Ignatius puts it this way: "For just as in consolation the good spirit guides and counsels us, so in desolation the evil spirit guides and counsels. Following his counsels we can never find the way to a right decision" (*SE*, Rules, First Week, #5)

When a person is in desolation, all objectivity is gone. The false spirit is her counselor—presenting foolish proposals, drawing incorrect conclusions, and making poor judgments. We get a medical checkup when we're in good health, not when experiencing acute illness or injury. Once, in order to do hospital ministry, one of our novices had to have a routine tuberculosis test. But he came down with a virus on the day he was to take the test. He was not able to take the test because the virus, which had no relation to tuberculosis, might have made the results look as if he did have the disease.

This is a great metaphor for what often happens in the spiritual life. A person in desolation draws conclusions about aspects of her life that are completely unrelated to the cause of the desolation. A young married person in desolation may interpret his sudden distance from his wife as a sign that the marriage is in trouble. Theresa's loneliness caused her to conclude that her father needed her back home. Noah's sadness caused him to believe that he was not fasting properly. Discernment during periods of desolation often yields very poor results. Therefore, the person in desolation cannot trust the notions that come to her during that period. Instead, she needs to lean more heavily on her support network for the decisions that must be made for the time being and wait until she is in the light of consolation to work toward lasting resolutions.

If consolation is the ideal time to work on desolations, then why are we so hesitant to do so? Often we hesitate to look at the painful parts of life because we're using the defense mechanism of avoidance. The psyche is programmed to fear psychological pain. We engage in avoidance in order to pretend that the problems do not exist. But we have already seen that fear is not a preferred tool of the true spirit. It's not wise to act out of fear—even if the action is to *avoid* doing something that would help. And to pretend that desolation won't come again is to remain naive and unprepared. Ignatius is blunt about this: "When one enjoys consolation, let him consider how he will conduct himself during the time of ensuing desolation, and store up a supply of strength as defense against that day" (*SE*, Rules, First Week, #10).

Spiritual writer Timothy Gallagher points out that Ignatius does not say that desolation *may* come after; he says definitively that desolation *will* come after. It is part of the human experience to have desolation from time to time; we have no choice about that. What we can choose is whether to prepare for the next time it comes. We can use the strength that comes from consolation—from closeness to God and from increased faith, hope, and love—to face the future with eyes wide open.

At our Jesuit Vow Ceremony in August 2003, our provincial, Father Fred Kammer, gave a stirring homily addressed to the men who were about to promise perpetual poverty, chastity, and obedience in the Society of Jesus. This is what he said:

> In the years to come,
>
> You will be tempted from poverty and simplicity—
>> to become more comfortable, to possess more things
>> to rely more on your degrees or positions or possessions
> than upon the gracious goodness of God,
>
> You will be tempted from fidelity and solitude—
>> to become ambiguous
>> to borrow intimacy in easy places,
>> to rationalize promiscuity
> rather than to walk with Jesus the Companion
> into the unknown darkness that is discipleship.
>
> You will be tempted from availability and obedience
>> to decide that you are needed in only one place,
>> that you alone know where God is calling you and
>> that no one appreciates the many gifts you have
> rather than to be ready and willing to go wherever you are called.

Wouldn't it have been better for Father Kammer to simply speak sweet and happy sentiments on this joyous occasion? Why would he make such unpleasant predictions? Anyone who has tried to live the vows—be they marriage vows or religious vows—knows why he spoke these words. He did so because they are true! He wisely and lovingly wanted these men to profess vows with their eyes wide open, and he wanted them to use the graces that come from the virtuous act of taking vows in order to fortify themselves for the days when the path will get steeper and the way forward will become more obscure. As unpleasant as it may be, this is our task when we are riding high in consolation: we prepare for the day when we will come down from those heights.

What, then, are some concrete ways to prepare for desolation while in consolation?

Preparation 1:
Observe the "Course of the Thoughts"

We must carefully observe the whole course of our thoughts. If the beginning and middle and end of the course of thoughts are wholly good and directed to what is entirely right, it is a sign that they are from the good angel. But the course of thoughts suggested to us may terminate in something evil, or distracting, or less good than the soul had formerly proposed to do. Again, it may end in what weakens the soul, or disquiets it; or by destroying the peace, tranquility, and quiet which it had before, it may cause disturbance to the soul. These things are a clear sign that the thoughts are proceeding from the evil spirit, the enemy of our progress and eternal salvation.

—SE, Rules for Discernment of Spirits, Second Week, #5

When the enemy of our human nature has been detected and recognized by the trail of evil making his course and by the wicked end to which he leads us, it will be profitable for one who has been tempted to review immediately the whole course of the temptation. Let him consider the series of good thoughts, how they arose, how the evil one gradually attempted to make him step down from the state of spiritual delight and joy in which he was, till finally he drew him to his wicked designs. The purpose of this review is that once such an experience has been understood and carefully observed, we may guard ourselves for the future against the customary deceits of the enemy.

—Rules, Second Week, #6

Once I have "detected and recognized by the trail of evil" the false spirit and have ascended out of the pit of desolation, Ignatius instructs me to go back and follow the course of thoughts that led me into the desolation.

111

What was the perceivable beginning of my desolation? What was my state of being just before that? What were my life circumstances around that time? Were there any exterior shifts that could have caused interior disquietude? Did anything upset me at that time? Did anything excite me or make me happy? Were there any important moments in my significant relationships?"

Ignatius suggests I pay special attention to thoughts: *What was on my mind back then? Any significant ideas or insights? Any shifts in my reasoning process?* I then ponder these same questions in regard to my emotions and actions. I go step-by-step through the process and detect even the slightest shifts. It may be that I find a subtle train of thoughts, emotions, or actions that slowly led me down the path of desolation. It might be like a thread woven through the pre-desolation, the beginning, the middle, and the end. Discovering this thread could be a huge breakthrough in my pursuit of self-awareness.

Or perhaps it will not be a thread running through the entire experience but rather a knot—a blip—stuck at some definite point in the midst of an otherwise "normal" procession of thoughts, emotions, or actions. Maybe there was one particular moment in the midst of it all that really seemed to bring disquietude; fear; confusion; lack of faith, hope, and love; lack of the sense of God's nearness. Once I have found that one moment, I could put it under the microscope to learn from it. Was it a particular topic? Was it caused by some exterior occurrence? Was it the result of faulty reasoning?

Examining the history of my last period of desolation, I could observe the colors and contours of the desolation. What were the manifestations of desolation for me? What made it worse? What made it better? Of the characteristics of desolation described in chapter 2, which were present in my experience? Which were not present?

This investigation into the "course of the thoughts" is not the same as an examination of conscience. I am not looking to find where I have sinned. The desolation could have been caused by sin, but it's also very possible that I did not actually sin at any point along the way. It might even be the case that I didn't make any mistakes during the desolation. My objective in this investigation, then, is not to accuse myself of moral failings or of incompetence but rather to learn about the *particular* ways desolation typically enters my life so that I can be better prepared for the next time it begins to creep back in.

However, if I do discover some root sin or psychological vulnerability, it is now, in consolation, that I can work toward more lasting moral or psychological health. While I must attend to the immediate consequences of my vulnerabilities during desolation, I should explore the *underlying causes* of them while in consolation. While in desolation, I do what I need to quickly "plug the hole" so that more trouble doesn't come. While in consolation, I work on the *ground zero* of my vulnerabilities, and I work on more lasting solutions. If I am quick tempered during desolation, then I will have to wait until after I've calmed down to explore what's beneath the problem. If I am prone to obsessive worrying, then I explore the roots of that fear in therapy, not only when I'm overwhelmed but also when I am most at peace. If spending holiday time with the family drives me crazy, then I may want to discuss my issues with them after the holiday has passed and I'm feeling "normal" again.

Preparation 2:
Attend to Vulnerabilities

Ignatius recommends that I prayerfully explore the areas in which I am vulnerable to spiritual (and I would add emotional) attack. Using the metaphor of the false spirit as an enemy combatant, Ignatius has this to say:

> A commander and leader of an army will encamp, explore the fortifications and defenses of the stronghold, and attack at the weakest point. In the same way, the enemy of our human nature investigates from every side all our virtues, theological, cardinal, and moral. Where he find the defenses of eternal salvation weakest and most deficient, there he attacks and tries to take us by storm.
>
> —SE, RULES FOR DISCERNMENT OF SPIRITS, FIRST WEEK, #14

Often, desolation comes through the portal of one of my points of vulnerability. Desolation will push my buttons. If I am prone to rage, desolation will provide things for me to get angry about. If I have low self-esteem, it will have me fixate on and exaggerate some criticism I've received recently. If I'm lazy, the TV remote will beckon as I set out to pray. The more I'm aware of my own weaknesses, the more I'll be able to recognize when the false spirit is going after them. During consolation, when I am clearheaded, Ignatius encourages me to reflect about this. What are the fear starters and anger starters within me? What are the situations that play over and over in my head the false tapes of self-loathing, jealousy, pride, anger, or fear? I should identify the following:

- **Places:** Whenever I go to that office [or that home], I find myself getting petty, jealous, or fearful.
- **People:** I don't like who I am when I'm around this person.

- **Topics:** Whenever politics are brought up, I go ballistic.
- **Times:** I get lonely in the late nights when I can't sleep. I'm cranky in the morning before I've had my coffee.
- **Personal traits:** I am quick tempered [or too sensitive, or unemotional, or passive, or a worrywart].

Remember that the ultimate goal is to identify the movements within me. By identifying my "buttons," I will more readily see danger ahead of time and prepare for it.

Defense Mechanisms: Common Vulnerabilities

Psychology informs us that when humans feel hurt or threatened, it is in their biology to protect themselves from the perceived threat. Often, without my even being aware of it, my unconscious defense mechanisms kick in, and I find myself reacting in ways that are unhealthy or unholy. Reflecting on inner experiences in light of the most common defense mechanisms may help me identify where I am most vulnerable.

- **Passivity and avoidance:** I feel frightened or threatened, and it paralyzes me. I suddenly find myself avoiding the uncomfortable situation. I participate less in the outside world and passively watch events occur rather than actively play a role in them. For example, if I find myself suddenly "forgetting" to meet with my mentor, it could be a form of avoidance.
- **Aggression:** Like a cat in the corner, I respond to hurt, criticisms, or threats by lashing out at people I perceive to be my enemies. I make preemptive strikes without proper discernment.

- **Passive-aggressive behavior:** This is a very common defense mechanism among adults who see passivity or aggressiveness as beneath them. Instead of a direct attack against my perceived enemy, I quietly sabotage his efforts. For example, my boss confronts me about something, and I concede the point. Then, behind his back, I make a joke about him to my coworkers, or I reveal something about him that would embarrass him. I might also suddenly have trouble finishing some project I know he's waiting on.
- **Displacement:** I direct my response to someone other than the person who has elicited the response. For example, I am hurt and angered by my wife, but I take it out on the kids instead. I shift, or displace, the negative feelings I have for someone or something that I can't change toward someone or something I can, even if this new object of my attention had nothing to do with the initial response.
- **Repression:** I deny, even to myself, any negative feelings that might be deemed unacceptable. Men often repress feelings of rejection or loneliness because they are perceived as signs of weakness. Women sometimes repress anger because they are taught that they are supposed to be docile and obedient.

Members of Alcoholics Anonymous learn that, even more basic than these defense mechanisms, simple human urgings sometimes compel us to do stupid things. When a recovering alcoholic is tempted to drink, she is taught to "HALT" and ask herself if some basic human need is not being met: Am I **h**ungry? **a**ngry? **l**onely? or **t**ired?

It's important to remember that often, without my knowing it, my unconscious is reacting to some threat, hurt, or need. The more I bring these problems into the level of consciousness in my prayer, the less likely will desolation use them to get the best of me.

Figure 4: Building Fortifications
1. I name the weak spots in me. In prayer, I bring to God the areas of my life where I struggle with these emotional potholes. I tell God in my prayer, "Lord, my sister really gets under my skin." "Lord, I noticed that I turn to food when I'm down." "Lord, jealousy of my coworker led me to gossip about him." "Lord, I took my schoolwork problems home with me today and snapped at my dad." I ask the Lord for insight and for healing.
2. I bring my weak spots to my support network. I admit the problem to my best friend and ask him to keep me accountable—to help me keep it in check. I ask my spiritual director for guidance on how I might pray about this point of vulnerability. I do some spiritual reading on this topic.
3. If appropriate, I tell the others about this vulnerability. This may be a painful or embarrassing revelation, but part of the role of a spouse, a family member, or a companion is to cover for my weak spots and to encourage me in those areas. Once, in the middle of my teasing him about something, my friend said to me, "I'm sensitive about that so don't tease me." I honestly had no idea beforehand and was so grateful to him for sharing that with me. Needless to say, I never teased him again in that area. In fact, I made a point to strengthen him by complimenting him when appropriate. This friend was wise and courageous in working on this vulnerability by telling me about it.
4. I commit myself to pray during the times when I feel especially vulnerable. I go directly to prayer during moments of tension; just before visiting the in-laws, while on my way to the job interview, before I sit down to eat, when I'm asked to do some work that I normally avoid.
5. I ask the Lord to help me move slowly and deliberately through the tense moments. I keep in mind that desolation often leads me to make imprudent changes and that my buttons often lead me to fly off the handle. I ask the Lord to help me to avoid unreflective reactions to stressful moments.
6. I choose to be proactive rather than reactive. For example, before my neighbor brings up politics, I tell myself that I'll really hear him out this time. I lead the conversation by affirming him on some point he made the last time we talked. Or, for another example, if I am shy and tend to avoid social situations, I pray for the grace to commit to staying at my friend's party a little longer than I normally would.

Preparation 3:
Look Out for False Consolation

I must look out for false consolation *when in desolation* because it is an easy though delusional escape from the pain. I must look out for false consolation *when in consolation* because it feels the same as true consolation, and I can slip into it without even noticing.

In the eighth rule, Ignatius speaks about a particular type of consolation called **consolation without previous cause**. This is an extraordinary type of consolation in which God consoles a person in a more direct way through a sort of mystical experience rather than as a consequence of a particular external occurrence or internal "course of thoughts." Ignatius explains, "I say without cause, without any previous sentiment or knowledge of some object, through which such a consolation comes." I have chosen not to explore this topic in great detail in this book for two reasons. First, there is a variety of interpretations (and little agreement) among Ignatian scholars as to the characteristics, frequency, and implications of this type of consolation. Second, Ignatius says of this experience that one does not need to discern since "it is of God our Lord alone to give consolation to the soul without preceding cause," and therefore, "there is no deception in it." Ignatius is saying that in this extraordinary moment of grace, God himself will be your guide and will lead you by the hand. This being true, there is little that needs to be said about it in a book on discernment.

However, Ignatius does give an important cautionary note in the eighth rule:

> But a spiritual person who has received such a consolation must consider it very attentively, and must cautiously distinguish the actual time of the consolation from the period which follows it. At such a time the soul is still fervent and favored with the grace and aftereffects of the

consolation which has passed. In this second period the soul frequently forms various resolutions and plans which are not granted directly by God our Lord. They may come from our own reasoning on the relations of our concepts and on the consequences of our judgments, or they may come from the good or evil spirit. Hence, they must be carefully examined before they are given full approval and put into execution.

—SE, RULES FOR DISCERNMENT OF SPIRITS, SECOND WEEK, #8

Sometimes, immediately following consolation without previous cause, the person is susceptible to false consolation. I would like to make an assertion that goes further than Ignatius's insight. On the basis of my own experience as a pray-er and as a spiritual director, I assert that a person is susceptible to false consolation immediately after *any* intense religious experience, whether it has a previous cause or not. To put it another way: *the more intense the experience of consolation, the more susceptible I am to false consolation immediately following.*

Sometimes the intoxicating consolation that immediately follows a profound experience—an intense religious retreat, a conversion or reconversion, a near-death or other mystical experience—will move a person to do something spiritually bold but not very prudent. For example, after a life-changing religious retreat, a young person might, without thorough discernment, attempt to join a monastery or become a lay missionary in Africa. A person might make an impossible commitment to pray several hours a day rather than pay attention to his or her ordinary vocations or family obligations. Ignatius, therefore, warns the retreat director:

If the one giving the Exercises sees that the exercitant is going on in consolation and in great fervor, he must admonish him not to be inconsiderate or hasty in making any promise or vow.

—SE, ANNOTATION 14

It bears repeating that the intense negative emotions that usually accompany desolation (for example, fear, anger, sadness) will lead a person to lose objectivity. It is also sometimes true that the extreme *positive* emotions following an intense experience of consolation (for example, ecstatic joy, extreme confidence, radical devotion) might also cause a loss in objectivity. While consolation is a good time to discern and act boldly, we should never do so without considering it "very carefully." All our actions, even those springing from consolation, should be "carefully examined" (#8).

Preparation 4:
Seek God's Presence in the Painful Moments of Your Past

When in desolation, I am often incapable of sensing God's presence in my life. During those difficult periods, I must simply choose to believe that God is present, even though I have no evidence. During consolation, then, it is important to *look back* on those dark moments in order to recognize the hand of God in them. One of the chief characteristics of consolation is the ease with which a person can "find God in all things," to use an Ignatian phrase. Looking backward to see how God was with me, guiding me, loving me all along, will increase the joy of consolation and help me act in faith—confidence in God's presence—the next time I am in desolation.

Receiving the Whole Story

As a gift from his parishioners, Duy Nguyen, a Vietnamese diocesan priest, made a thirty-day Ignatian retreat. The first few days, Father Duy spent simply praising God for his life, which was fulfilling and enriching. He had good friends and good relationships with his congregation. His relationship with God had grown only stronger over the years. More than anything, he rejoiced over the precious gift of the priesthood. Looking back on his fifteen years as a priest, Duy found that nothing made him feel more fully human and fully alive than the times he was able to be Christ for the people who came to him for priestly help.

As the retreat days stretched on, however, Duy went further back in his memory to his violent and traumatic escape from Vietnam and to the harrowing sea voyage to America. This experience had left a deep wound that he knew he would carry to his grave. The more he meditated on this wound, the greater the anger he felt at God for letting him experience this. For two full days of prayer, God seemed to be silent while Duy asked, "Why, Lord?" over and over again. Finally, on the third day of praying over his tragic experience, he felt a strong sense of God's healing presence. Although God seemed to give no answer to Duy's question, still, God's warm embrace was a balm for the open wounds. Duy had no more answers than the day before, and yet he experienced a quiet, soothing consolation.

On the fourth day, God seemed to lead Duy in an imaginative exercise. God offered to give Duy a little peek at the divine plan played out in his priestly life. Duy saw one scene after another of his ministering to God's people in extraordinary ways. He watched as he brought spiritual healing and relief to so many through the sacrament of reconciliation and through pastoral counseling.

As in the first few days of his retreat, he was flooded with joy and gratitude for these experiences. But this second time around, God showed him precisely how Duy's tragic past played a role in his priesthood. For the first time in his life, Duy noticed how much he unconsciously used his painful past to get in touch with the pain of those he counseled. He seldom spoke of his tragedy during those sessions, but every word he exchanged with them, every tear he shed with them, every prayer he shared with them, came from the common human experience of God's steadfast love in the midst of tragedy. There was one couple in particular who had lost their nine-year-old boy in a freak accident. The couple came to see Duy often during their long bouts of grief. Though they had little in common (the couple were white Americans from wealthy backgrounds), the three of them bonded in the pain, tears, and prayers. It was the most important and fulfilling experience of Duy's priestly life, and he could see clearly now how his own tragic past played a necessary role in the healing process of this couple's grief.

In Duy's prayerful imagination, God said to him, "I am almighty and all powerful. If you ask me to, I will take you back in time to your birth and remove the entire tragic experience of your immigration to America. I will replace it with an easier, less painful past." Duy thought about all that God had done with his wounded past—how God had somehow found a way to make it an instrument of salvation for himself and for those to whom he ministered. He saw clearly how integral his tragedy was in the most important moments of his adulthood, and especially of his priesthood. He turned to God, with tears streaming down his face, and said, "No, thank you, Lord. I'll keep it all."

It was the most joyful moment of his life.

Two Helpful Practices

We have easy access to two practices that can greatly help us prepare for future times of desolation. Both are means of processing our experiences and reflecting on them. From our reflection comes wisdom; in fact, reflection is a key emphasis in Ignatian practice, because only when we reflect on our experience can we engage our interior life effectively and learn from it.

The first practice is *spiritual direction and/or mentorship*. Let us not be like the adolescents I mentioned earlier, who came for counseling only as a means of putting out fires but never came for fire prevention. When we feel strong, healthy, and happy, we are tempted to discontinue our visits with directors and mentors. We think that because we're fine, we no longer need those visits. But Ignatius would beg to differ. If we're really going to work on reviewing the past desolation, on shoring up vulnerabilities, on looking out for false consolation, and on seeking God in the painful parts of the past, we will need the objectivity that only someone on the outside of the experience can provide. There are simply too many temptations for denial and avoidance as we work on these touchy areas of life.

Spiritual journaling is the second helpful practice when preparing for desolation. One of the difficulties of working with vulnerabilities, desolations, and painful past events is the lack of clear thinking that often accompanies these experiences—we might think of walking through a fog as an accurate description. Consolation might allow for clearer thinking and reasoning, but even from this better viewpoint, objective reasoning can be difficult. Writing out our reflections in a journal can be helpful because it is a visual process rather than simply a mental one. Sketching the step-by-step descent into the most recent desolation, for example, might be easier to do if we sketch out on paper the progression of thoughts. Some people find it helpful to draw pictures or diagrams, another way to work visually with the interior life.

Figure 5: Four Ways to Prepare for Desolation
1. Observe the course of thoughts.
2. Look out for false consolation.
3. Attend to vulnerabilities.
4. Seek God in your painful past.

Another purpose for journaling while in consolation is the simple gathering of evidence. It is in consolation when we see things as they really are—that is, we are able to see the goodness of God's creation inside us and all around us. Our assessments of relationships, of our own strengths and gifts, and of our friendship with God will be far more accurate during consolation than during desolation. Setting down these assessments in a journal will provide documentation of the good qualities in our lives. If I am writing down what I perceive while in consolation, then I'll have something to return to the next time I'm in desolation and my assessments become dark and cloudy. And just as I will be tempted to neglect spiritual direction when all is well, so might I be attracted to journaling only when times are tough. I might therefore need to make a concrete commitment to journal not only when I am in crisis but also when I am experiencing consolation.

Prayer Exercise B: Observing Past Desolation

Begin your prayer time by placing yourself in an alert but comfortable position. Spend a good while quieting yourself and asking the Spirit of God to be present to you and to fill you with life. Soak in the spirit as you would soak in a warm bath.

If you feel called to do so, begin to reflect on a time when the false spirit got the best of you. It could be an ordinary time when you snapped at your spouse or your spouse snapped at you, or it could be a more lasting and critical time when the "bad space" you were in led to deeper distress. As painful as it may be to do so, go back to that moment and feel what you felt at that time. Feel the anger, the hurt, and so on. Keep in mind, though, that you are not now in that bad space and therefore you have nothing to fear or worry about. It is in this good space that you can look back at that bad moment and learn from it. Here are a few ways that you might reflect on moments of desolation while you bask in the grace of consolation.

- What tricks did the false spirit play on you while you were in desolation? What false presumption were you led to believe? What were the predominant emotions? In particular, were there any fears that got the best of you? Was the experience of desolation prolonged by your being fed by or by your feeding the false spirit? Speak with God about this.

- Remaining in the good space of God's love, ask God to show you the points of vulnerability in your life. What are the places, people, topics, times, and situations that set you off down a bad road? Note each of them in your journal. Take each of these to God. Speak with God about each, and if you feel called to do so, ask God for healing. Mostly, just sit in the warmth of God's unconditional love.

- Look back on bad moments in your life and note if there were times when you resisted the call to share your problems with a caring person. Recognize the relief, healing, and consolation you received when you finally did talk it over with someone. Speak to God about this.

- Look over your life and consider whether there was ever a time when the false spirit came as an "angel of light." That is, was there ever a time when going down a particular path seemed beautiful and right but turned out to be a dead end? Ask God to teach you about that moment so that you can recognize similar times in the future. Review what happened back then and ask God to reveal any telltale signs of the false spirit that you can look out for in the future.

- Look back at the desolate moments of your life and see that God used even those hard times to give you spiritual gifts like courage, fortitude, humility, and love. Observe God's presence in your most desolate moments, leading you and upholding you though you did not recognize God in the midst of it.

The purpose of these exercises is not to make you feel bad or guilty or to depress you but rather to ask that the light of Christ might help you observe and learn from experiences of desolation so that you might be less susceptible to them in the future.

Ready for Discernment

Part 1 introduced St. Ignatius and showed how the events of his life led to his conversion and to his lifelong fascination with discernment. It introduced the concepts of the false spirit and the accompanying desolation, and the true spirit and its accompanying consolation and gave characteristics of them both.

Part 2 presented concrete suggestions for how a person can respond to the experiences of desolation and consolation in everyday life. In chapter 4 we dealt with eight ways of responding to desolation, in chapter 5, four ways of responding to consolation.

But we have not yet explored the *most* important ways of responding to consolation: praising, reverencing, and serving God. Praise and reverence are fairly self-explanatory and come naturally when we're in consolation. The tricky part is discerning how, when, and where to serve.

What are my vocations in life—what am I called to do with my life? Note that the word *vocations* is plural here; we are searching for ways to discern our big vocations such as marriage, single life, or religious life, but we are also interested in our smaller vocations: *Where am I called to live? Who am I called to befriend? What work am I called to do and where?* And we are even interested in how we might discern the smaller stuff that comes up in the course of a day: *Should I confront the boss about this? Should I work on this little project or that one? Should I steer our group into moving in this direction or that one? Should I call in sick today or buck up and go to work?*

Having begun to explore the world of consolations and desolations, we can now put that knowledge to work as we discern these big and small callings in life. Ignatius offers a lot of pithy and wise advice about how to use discernment of spirits to consider the various questions that arise in the course of a typical life. This is the subject of part 3.

Chapter 6 presents the disposition one must have before beginning the process of discernment and introduces the important concept of Ignatian

Indifference. Chapter 7 returns to the conversion story of St. Ignatius and uses that story as a template for the four phases that usually accompany a good discernment. Chapter 8 presents the penultimate act of offering one's tentative decision to God and of awaiting confirmation of that decision. Provided that the person has received that confirmation, he or she is ready to make the final decision. The book concludes, then, with suggestions on how to enact a final decision and on how to avoid the pitfalls that sometimes follow after a final decision is enacted.

PART 3

From Discerning Spirits to Making Decisions

If St. Ignatius was correct in saying that I should not make a decision when in desolation, then it follows that I *should* discern and act during a time of consolation. This, then, is the time to decide what exactly God is calling me to do at a particular juncture in my life. But how do I make that decision? With so many choices before me, how do I decide what is my specific calling?

The world is full of good people trying to do the right thing. But how does a person determine what is exactly the right thing to do in his or her particular circumstance? Sometimes a person is faced with more than one good option, which presents a problem, because then the person is left to determine the *better* choice.

Every day, each one of us makes multiple decisions. Many of them are not well reasoned but are simply what we perceive to be the most comfortable path. Many aren't decisions at all but our avoidance of decision making until circumstances force one outcome or another. Some decisions are the product of careful consideration and deliberation, but few—very few—come out of a process of prayerful discernment.

I believe that most people really do want to make wise decisions. In fact, many sincere people would love to make their decisions prayerfully, but they feel completely lost as to how to do that. This part of the book is designed to help those people make good choices.

6

Before Making a Decision: Laying a Foundation

In his classic work *The Spiritual Exercises*, St. Ignatius of Loyola lays out the path a soul takes as it seeks and finds God. It was the path taken by Ignatius's own soul: the journey—

- from sin and guilt to redemption and mercy
- from creation to incarnation to resurrection
- from gratitude to service and back again to awestruck gratitude for God's love permeating and laboring through all creation.

But before describing this journey, in just a few paragraphs Ignatius sets down what he calls the First Principle and Foundation. Only recently have organizations, both religious and secular, discovered the importance of identifying and articulating a first principle and foundation. In vestibules of churches across America and on the home pages of corporations and organizations across the Internet, we encounter the mission statement. If it is a strong and well-articulated statement, all the organization's actions will flow from and return to that statement. The mission statement—or, in Ignatian language, the principle and foundation—is the essential grounding of an organization's, or a person's, meaning and activity.

First Principle and Foundation
Man is created to praise, reverence, and serve God our Lord, and by this means to save his soul.

The other things on the face of the earth are created for man to help him in attaining the end for which he is created.

> Hence, man is to make use of them in as far as they help him in the attainment of his end, and he must rid himself of them in as far as they prove a hindrance to him.
>
> Therefore, we must make ourselves indifferent to all created things, as far as we are allowed free choice and are not under any prohibition. Consequently, as far as we are concerned, we should not prefer health to sickness, riches to poverty, honor to dishonor, a long life to a short life. The same holds for all other things.
>
> Our one desire and choice should be what is more conducive to the end for which we are created.
>
> —SE, P. 12

Before making a big decision, I, too, want to set down for myself the foundation, the very purpose of the actions I am presently discerning. If I am a working woman who is considering resigning my job in order to be a stay-at-home mom, I ask, *What is most important to me? What is best for my children, and how do I provide that for them?* If I am a lawyer considering my next career move, I begin the discernment by asking, *Why am I a lawyer in the first place? Why has God called me to this work? What is my purpose as a lawyer in the grand scheme of things?* If I am an elderly woman in a retirement home, feeling lost and depressed, I contemplate, *What might God be calling me to in these last years of my life? How might I contribute to my small world of family, friends, and nursing home community?* If I am a teenager discerning what college to attend, I ask, *Why do I want to go to college in the first place? What is the purpose of a college education? With my higher degree, how might I give glory to God and be of service to my loved ones and to the global community?*

These are the big questions that will set the foundation for all other questions that follow. Keeping before her consciousness the grand design of her college life will transform the questions a teenager asks as she tours a college campus and writes her college essay. While teenagers who have not prayerfully set down a first principle are sizing up dorm rooms and counting the college-town bars in each neighborhood, perhaps a discerning teenager will be reading the college's mission statement and comparing it with her own life principles. While others might ask about boy-girl ratios and Internet access, she might ask about the school's commitment to justice and its record on admitting a diverse student body. Every subsequent step of the process of discernment will be formed and shaped by the way she sets down her first principle and foundation.

In this chapter we explore several questions and concepts that help shape a person's principle and foundation.

In every good choice, as far as depends on us, our intention must be simple. I must consider only the end for which I am created.

—SE, P. 71

What Do You Seek?

I can recall numerous situations in my own life for which asking the big questions transformed the whole discernment of small day-to-day decisions and of enormous life-changing decisions as well. Years ago, having relocated to another city to begin a new assignment, I found myself struggling to decide whom to seek out as my new spiritual director. One evening on the way to a movie with my friend Jim, I told him of my grappling to decide which person to approach. Jim asked a simple question: "What are you looking for at this time in your life?" That question changed everything! One might think that I would have begun my discernment with such a question, but instead I had leapfrogged this vital first question and went straight to secondary questions such as, "What are the qualities of this person?" and "How well will I get along with that person?"

First principle and foundation: The statement that answers the big questions about the purpose of my life and the purpose of this decision.

But when Jim asked that basic question, it was easy to see why I couldn't make a decision. Even if I knew the qualities and characteristics of each potential director, how would I choose the direction if I hadn't even determined the specific goals of direction? What was my *purpose* in seeking out such a person in the first place? Asking myself Jim's big question in prayer, I quickly identified the right person to approach.

Many years ago, when I was a young Jesuit preparing for priesthood, I fell in love with a lay student at the school I was attending. After weeks of turbulent emotions, I had an epiphany in prayer one day when I heard myself say to Jesus, "Nothing is more important to me than living my vowed commitment to you, Lord." Though it was many years ago, I can still clearly recall the tremendous relief and joy I felt at that moment. In the midst of the disorientation of falling in love, I had found again my purpose, my principle and foundation. With prayer and a supportive network of friends, mentors, and the church, I then could take this experience of falling in love as the gift—the grace—that God meant it to be. Journeying through this relationship on the foundation of this first principle, I allowed God to form me into a better priest and a better man than I ever could have been had I denied having feelings for that person or if I had abandoned my vocation on the basis of those feelings.

Here is another example of how asking the big questions changes everything. Ray, the father of three boys, went to a Jesuit high school as a teenager and found it to be a life-changing experience. Years later, his two older sons, Paul and Brian, loved Ray's alma mater so much that the youngest son, Allen, couldn't wait to be old enough to go there himself. Meanwhile, Ray received a lucrative offer to relocate to a distant city. He sat with young Allen and explained the reasons they

> The two disciples . . . followed Jesus. When Jesus turned and saw them following, he said to them, "What are you looking for?" They said to him, "Rabbi" (which translated means Teacher), "where are you staying?" He said to them, "Come and see."
>
> —JOHN 1:37–39

might be moving out of Houston. Allen listened patiently and with interest. When Ray had finished his explanations, Allen asked, "That's fine, Dad, but I still get to go to a Jesuit school, right?" This made Ray rethink his decision. His current job provided more than enough for them to live comfortably, so why was he considering a move? For his children's happiness? But what are the things that would *really* make Allen and the other children happy? Pondering these bigger questions ultimately led Ray to turn down the offer.

And still another example, if on a smaller scale: Lupe felt underappreciated at work. As her annual job-performance review approached, she grew increasingly more anxious. However, when the big day arrived, her boss called her into the office, gave her a glowing review, and said, "Lupe, we love your work." Lupe was thrilled and couldn't wait to tell the story to her best friend, Mary Carmen, at their weekly supper out. But when she arrived at the restaurant, she immediately knew that something was wrong. Mary Carmen was crying profusely as she reached out to hug Lupe. "Thomas dumped me!" she wailed. So, the whole evening was spent processing Mary Carmen's traumatic experience. Lupe wanted badly to share her good news, but she decided that Mary Carmen's needs outweighed her own wants. Lupe's principle and foundation included sharing Christ's love, to the best of her ability, in every circumstance. She would wait to share her good news on another day.

Prayer Exercise C: Principle and Foundation

At this early stage, you tap into the great big desires of your heart, starting with the desire to praise, reverence, and serve God our Lord and to have Jesus as your intimate companion. Your prayer time should be grounded in longing to be with Christ—to love him, to praise him, and to serve him.

- In prayer, recall early experiences of Christ calling you to his side and of your responses to that call. Prayerfully remember the moment you committed your life to Christ in some concrete way, through moments of conversion, through a retreat or religious ceremony that moved you, through receiving one of the sacraments for the first time, through setting out to accomplish a momentous life goal such as learning a particular trade, through committing your life to your spouse or professing vows in a religious order. Sit quietly and relish these memories. Gratefully praise and reverence God for these life-changing moments.

- Steeped in gratitude for God's mercy and call, ask yourself the big questions: What is the purpose of life? What is the purpose of *my* life? What is it that gets me out of bed every morning? When I am old and near death, what sort of life would I be proud and happy to look back on?

- Perhaps two or three words or phrases will arise as you ponder these big questions, words such as *service, love, family, loyalty, God's glory, ultimate sacrifice, affirmation, saying yes, new beginnings, change for the better, fatherhood/motherhood, brotherhood/sisterhood, single-minded, true friend, faithful spouse, devotion,* and so on.

- Take these words and phrases and set down your own principle and foundation, your own mission statement. With paper and pen, or perhaps with paintbrush or guitar, articulate what you believe is your reason for being. Begin as Ignatius did, setting down the purpose for which God has created you. Write, "God has created me to . . ."

- Then move from this most basic statement to more particular and concrete vocations. For example, in my Jesuit life, I would begin with expressions of love and service to God and then move to my particular vocations: the Jesuits, the priesthood, writing, teaching, the formation of youths and beginners in religious life. If I were a layperson, I might begin with expressions of love and service of God and then move to my vocations as spouse and parent. My vocation to provide for my family leads me to my work as a lawyer. My vocation to teach my children the faith leads me to my vocation as church member. And so on. For each of the vocations you name, recall the moment God called you and the moment you said yes. Then articulate each of these vocations through a "God has created me to . . ." statement.

Later in the discernment process, take your principle and foundation statement and flesh it out even further, getting right down to the particular decision you're presently considering. But for now, keep it big, sweeping over the length and breadth of God's personal call to you—and your personal response.

A Grateful Heart

There's much diversity among the saints, mystics, and other spiritual heroes. They express a variety of personalities, gifts, and callings. But one characteristic that seems to permeate the prayers of them all is gratitude.

This is no less true of St. Ignatius of Loyola. His classic *Spiritual Exercises*, which is designed to guide a person through a thirty-day retreat, is chock-full of gratitude. At the beginning, I, the retreatant, am to reflect on the staggering, almost unbelievable notion that all the things of the earth were created with my benefit in mind—that God, billions of years before my birth, considered my personal needs and my unique desires while creating the universe. Later in the *Exercises*, I am to consider the Incarnation by imagining the Trinity looking down on the world and responding, not in anger, but out of compassion and mercy, deciding to incarnate God's very self into the world in order to heal it. Then I, the retreatant, follow Jesus through his life, death, and resurrection, marveling at all that Jesus did for me. Finally, near the very end, Ignatius asks me to reflect on how God labors through all the elements of creation— through cattle and trees, leaves and buildings, to communicate divine love for all creation, yes, but also to me, personally.

Even Ignatius's numerous meditations on sin ultimately lead the retreatant not to shame or self-loathing but to profound gratitude. Indeed, gratitude is the underlying grace Ignatius seeks for the repentant retreatant. He wishes for the retreatant to take a long sober look at her sinfulness precisely because it was in reflecting on Ignatius's own sinful past that he became smitten with the love and mercy of God.

And Ignatius had plenty of sins upon which to reflect! We have already seen how before his conversion he was a womanizer, gambler, drinker, and brawler. Shortly after his conversion, this sinful past left Ignatius in such despair that he considered killing himself. He had a profound sense of his own unworthiness and wondered "how it is that the earth did not open to swallow me up?" (*SE*, p. 30). But the more he prayed about his sins, the more he marveled at God's loving him unconditionally, and as time went on, Ignatius gradually gave God permission to heal him, renew him, and make him whole again. Knowing all too well his previous sinful state, and experiencing so profoundly the forgiveness of God for all these sins, Ignatius became the embodiment of gratitude.

"Cockeyed with gratitude"—as former poet laureate Billy Collins puts it—how would Ignatius respond to God? What can a person say and do in response to such breathtaking divine love? Offer it back to the Giver.

> Take, Lord, and receive
> all I have and call my own.
> You have given all to me.
> To you, Lord, I return it.
> Everything is yours;
> do with it what you will.

This is how Ignatius responded. This is the experience of all lovers. The beloved is so grateful for the self-gift of the lover that she gathers all that she's been given and offers it back to the lover.

The psalmist, filled with this grateful longing to give back all that he had received, dedicates his very life to God:

> What shall I return to the LORD
>> for all his bounty to me?
> I will lift up the cup of salvation
>> and call on the name of the LORD.
> I will pay my vows to the LORD
>> in the presence of all his people
>
> —PSALM 116:12–14

Such is the cycle of transcendent love: the recipient of the gifts becomes so grateful that he offers back those very gifts to the Giver. This mutual self-giving is at the very heart of the Eucharist: as the First Eucharistic Prayer for Children so beautifully puts it, "Change these gifts of bread and wine into the Body and Blood of Jesus Christ. *Then we can offer to you the gift you've given us.*"

Two Stories of Gratitude

After many barren years and lots of fervent prayers, Tamika finally became pregnant and delivered her first and only child, Samantha. One terrifying day, Tamika found baby Samantha sweating in her crib and convulsing uncontrollably. She and her husband, George, rushed the baby to the hospital. While George shakily filled out forms at the admitting window of the emergency room, Tamika held Samantha in her arms, closed her eyes and prayed, "Lord, you have given me this beautiful child. I beg you to keep her safe. She is your child. If she lives, I will forever offer her back to you." Samantha did indeed survive and went on to live a perfectly healthy life. Tamika was forever grateful to God for the gift of motherhood.

Years later, the twenty-five-year-old Samantha talked to her mom about her thoughts of becoming a religious sister. She was only considering it, she assured her mom, and she wanted to know what Tamika thought about it. Tamika's heart sank. For years, she longed for the day when she might have a house full of grandchildren. But as Samantha nervously waited to hear her mother's thoughts, Tamika remembered that fervent prayer in the emergency room years ago. She told that story to Samantha and said, "You and I belong to God, Samantha. If you and God want this, then I'm all for it, too."

I personally experienced this grateful offering up of my own life in the second year of my priesthood. By that time, my prayer life was saturated with gratitude. Practically all my life, I had longed to be a priest, and after thirteen years of formation as a Jesuit (we move very slowly!), I found myself finally with the unbelievable gift of administering the sacraments—giving God's holy things to God's holy people. And unlike most other experiences of extreme anticipation, this fulfillment of my lifelong dream was even more profound than I had imagined it. I loved everything about being a priest. I was so grateful to God for this gift that I found my heart responding with a *great desire* to spend my life praising and serving God. Nothing else was as important to me.

It was at that time that my provincial superior, Father Fred Kammer, asked me to pray about what might become my next assignment as a Jesuit priest. He gave me three or four assignments to consider and asked me to write a letter to him in a few weeks, sharing the fruits of my prayer. Here is an excerpt from that letter:

> I have spent a significant amount of time thinking, praying, and conversing with friends about these possibilities for the future and feel ready to give you the fruit of these reflections. But the most important thing I have to share with you, Fred, is that from the moment of our conversation to this moment, I have been completely at peace about my future. I'm delighted to say to you that I feel ready and willing to do any of the works we discussed. (I'm a bit surprised by this great gift of indifference since, in the past, I have fretted a bit more than I should have over my future. But I will take this gift from God as just that and thank him for it.) So, Fred, please feel free to discern the needs of the Church and the province with the assurance that I'm ready to step in wherever you feel I would be of greater service. All of the points that I present below then, should be taken as random puzzle pieces to help you put it all together—as opposed to arguments from me to do one thing over another.

Prayer Exercise D: Praying with Gratitude

On a sheet of paper or perhaps in your journal, make a graffiti page of random gifts God has given you. Simply allow one gift after another to come to mind, and jot down each one, praising God for the gift.

Zero in on the one gift for which you are most grateful at this moment. It could be the simplest and most trivial of them all. Use that one gift as the springboard of your praise and thanks for all that God has done for you.

Reflect on why it is that you do good acts. Is it out of obligation, or fear of God? Or is it grateful response to God's goodness?

Reflect on Psalm 116. Prayerfully consider what would be a grateful response to God for all the good that God has given you. If you feel called to do so, make a vow to God to respond to his love in some particular and concrete way.

For God's Greater Glory

Four hundred and fifty years ago, St. Ignatius predicted that every soul that embarks on an honest journey and is open to the Spirit will find itself with this great desire to turn over one's entire life to God. That is why Ignatius began his First Principle and Foundation with these simple words: "[Human beings are] created to praise, reverence, and serve God our Lord."

Earlier, I said that every decision maker must begin discernment by asking the big questions—must set down for herself the foundation and purpose of all her actions. Ignatius was convinced that if the soul were truly in touch with its deepest desires, it would find itself wanting nothing more than to praise, reverence, and serve God—wanting nothing more than to glorify God with one's life. It is the deepest desire of all and is the ultimate source of all other desires. Once a person names that greatest desire of all, she then finds herself ready to give up whatever does not lead to the glory of God and ready to take on whatever will lead to the *greater* glory of God.

Even things that every human logically strives for—good health, financial security, good reputation, a long life—even these supposedly essential elements of life are not as important as God's glorification. For God's greater glory, the soul is ready to take on, or let go of, anything.

Ignatian Indifference

As I said in the letter to Father Kammer, this gratitude for the present and readiness to do anything to which God calls is indeed a precious gift that should be cherished when it comes. In fact, it's the most important gift a person could hope for in this process of discernment. The extent to which I have this gift is the extent to which I will gracefully and smoothly discern my next step.

Ignatian spirituality calls this gift of grateful availability **Ignatian indifference**. Obviously, this is quite different from what is normally referred to as indifference—that is, the negative attitude of not caring about something. On the contrary, Ignatian indifference is filled with passion—passion for the will of God and the good of all. If I am indifferent in this Ignatian sense, then I care so much about serving God in a quite definite way that I am willing and ready to take on anything—or give up anything—for the cause. Ignatian indifference does not ignore desires but rather taps into our deepest desire—our desire to praise, reverence, and serve God.

Here is what Ignatius said about indifference:

> We must make ourselves indifferent to all created things, as far as we are allowed free choice and are not under any prohibition. Consequently, as far as we are concerned, we should not prefer health to sickness, riches to poverty, honor to dishonor, a long life to a short life. The same holds for all other things.
>
> —*SE*, FIRST PRINCIPLE AND FOUNDATION, P. 12

Why is indifference so important to discernment? If I set out to make a decision without indifference, then I'll unconsciously be steering my discernment toward the option that I want. Why discern at all if I'm not actually open to more than one possibility? But to be indifferent, I am even more than open to other possibilities—I truly *desire* to follow *any* of the perceived paths so long as it leads to God's greater glory.

Indifference of the Heart,
Indifference of the Will

This gift of indifference necessarily is just that: a gift from God. I cannot manufacture indifference myself, no matter how hard I try. It would be great if my whole self, my heart and my will, had this sense of indifference. But if, at any given moment, I do not have *indifference of the heart*, then all is not lost. I can simply pray for and work toward *indifference of the will*. In other words, in any given moment of discernment, I may not have the *feelings* of indifference but nevertheless willfully choose the path of indifference.

For example, if discerning whether to take a teaching job in Birmingham or in Kansas City, I may want—on an emotional level—to go to one city over another. But in my prayer, I tap into my gratitude for God's gracious gift of teaching and into my deeper desire to serve in whatever way brings about God's greater glory. With my own will, I make a choice to ground myself in that deeper desire for God's greater glory rather than in any superficial inclination to live in one city or another. I can choose this deeper desire of serving God in whatever location will bring about God's greater glory and allow the more superficial desire of one city over another simply to be another desire that happens to be in me at the time. This is the entire point of laying down a principle and foundation: I choose that which aides me in achieving the end for which I am created: praise, reverence, and service to God.

Ignatian indifference: The grace-filled state of desiring to do God's will and to praise, reverence and serve God more than desiring anything else. The state of grateful availability.

It isn't that my inclinations (for one city over another, for example) are bad. Those inclinations may well be coming from the true spirit—they could turn out to be a crucial sign of God's will for me. For this reason, I will want to spend good-quality time praying over those inclinations *later on*. But for now, at this beginning point of the discernment process, I want to attend to my principle and foundation. I want to set down for myself the purpose of who I am; I want to see my actions in the larger context of God's action in the world. Only after I have grounded myself in that greater purpose will I be ready to weigh my inclinations, thoughts, desires, and so on.

> It is necessary to keep as my aim the end for which I am created, that is, the praise of God our Lord and the salvation of my soul. Besides this, I must be indifferent, without any inordinate attachment, so that I am not more inclined or disposed to accept the object in question than to relinquish it, nor to give it up than to accept it. I should be like a balance at equilibrium, without leaning to either side, that I might be ready to follow whatever I perceive is more for the glory and praise of God our Lord and for the salvation of my soul.
>
> —SE, P. 75

7

Deciding: Four Phases to Good Discernment

During the process of writing this book, I came to see how Ignatius was not so much interested in creating a foolproof, step-by-step manual for decision making but wanted to shape the kind of person who could intuitively sense the spirits of the movements within her and thereby could know God's will. Ignatius was interested in building not a *process* of discernment but rather a *person* of discernment. Once a person has developed this **Ignatian intuition**, discernment will flow more naturally and smoothly.

Ignatian intuition: The internal ability to perceive the movements of the two spirits within me.

Rather than presenting a step-by-step cookbook sort of process for discerning, I provide here a more organic progression. I lay down the pattern that tends to flow within the process of good discernment. I use Ignatius's own conversion story as a sort of prototype for the way a discerning person tends to discern.

Recall St. Ignatius's story from chapter 1. It all began with the shattering of Ignatius's leg and his consequent convalescence. While stuck in bed for months, Ignatius began to read religious books informing his imagination of what it might be like to follow Christ closely and to live like the saints. With this new "data," he began to stumble accidently into

151

a sort of quiet prayer in which he would imagine himself living as a soldier of Christ—living as did St. Francis and St. Dominic. He dreamed other daydreams, too, of living a nobleman's chivalric life. These two contrasting sets of dreams occupied a great deal of his time and psychic energy. After a while, he began to ponder what his internal reaction to those two sets of dreams might mean. In reflecting on them, he began to sense the roots of the desires that welled up within him as he daydreamed, and from this pondering, he discovered a way to come to know the will of God.

Using this progression of Ignatius's conversion as a template, let's explore the phases that a typical discernment tends to follow. In making a good discernment, a person typically will

- get quiet
- gather data
- dream dreams
- ponder the dreams.

Phase 1:
Get Quiet

But our Lord restored his health, and he grew better. He was healthy in every respect except that he could not readily stand on that leg, and he was thus forced to remain in bed.

AUTOBIOGRAPHY, 44

The modern world, for all its marvels, is simply too noisy for our own good. We cannot think straight with the cacophony of competing values presented by advertisements, the media, politicians, and the people around us. In order to hear the sound of God's voice, we must turn down the sound of the world. We must come to a place of stillness within by separating ourselves from the noise outside. Even for an experienced discerner, the movements of the spirits are simply too subtle to detect without quieting down for a little while each day.

It took a cannonball to quiet down Ignatius's life enough for him to consider an alternative from that of soldier and womanizer. We hope that quieting down ourselves will not require such a drastic event! All we need is a small commitment to pray every day and the internal self-discipline to keep that commitment.

> According to Quaker tradition, anyone at any time can call for silence.

I need a consistent and meaningful prayer life.

By definition, discernment is all about prayer. If I am to discern well, I must have a **prayer life**. Having a prayer life involves more than simply praying every day. It is

> When we are alone and quiet, we fear that something will be whispered into our ear, and for this reason we hate the quiet and drug ourselves with social life.
>
> —FRIEDRICH NIETZSCHE

a core experience of my day-to-day life. Prayer does not necessarily take up a lot of my time, but it does take up a lot of my interior space, in terms of its impact on the whole of my life. I understand prayer as crucial to my well-being. When a companion sincerely asks "How are you?" the state of my prayer life will be an important part of my answer. It is almost as if my prayer life were a person with whom I am in a loving relationship: I care for it, nurture it, and give my whole heart to it. My prayer life, in turn, nurtures me, grounds me, and gives me direction. Sad to say, I also neglect my prayer life. I get bored with it and tussle with it. Sometimes we just don't get along. But I am always in relationship with it.

Prayer life: Through prayer, my ongoing intimate relationship with God.

A prayer life doesn't have to be mystical, beautiful, or inspirational. Even to seasoned pray-ers this spiritual habit often seems quite ordinary and uneventful. What is crucial is the prayer's importance to the one doing the praying. All that matters is that a person pray a little every day in order to grow closer to the God, who very dearly desires to grow closer to that person.

> Discernment remains obscure and mysterious to most pray-ers; and this despite the fact that, as I believe, discernment is the essential link between prayer and the active Christian life, the meeting point of prayer and apostolic action.
>
> —Thomas H. Green, *Weeds Among the Wheat*

In the end, what I say or what I think God says, what Scripture passages I use, or what positions I sit in don't matter very much. What matters is that I am reaching out to God. I can trust that God will take care of the rest. Methods and postures are logistical details that help a beginner get started, but praying is not like brain surgery. If I'm sincere, I can't really mess it up.

So what are these logistical details?

I don't need to pray for long stretches of time every day, but I do need to pray a little *every* day.

Very few people have the luxury of praying for long periods, and frankly, it isn't necessary. If I am a beginner, I could start with ten or fifteen minutes and very gradually build up to thirty or thirty-five. It's more important that I make it a habit and not skip many days. It is better to pray consistently for fifteen minutes a day than to pray an hour only every now and then.

Concretely, what do I do during my prayer time?

There are many step-by-step guides for beginners in prayer, including my own book *Armchair Mystic*. I recommend getting one of these and working through it with a mentor who has been praying awhile. Basically, this is what usually happens in daily prayer:

1. Before beginning prayer, I think about what has been on my mind and heart these days, what I might want to pray about. I set beside me anything that might help me focus on this matter: a Scripture passage, a spiritual reading, a photograph, the brochure of the college I hope to attend, a journal entry, my wedding ring.

2. I begin with some formulaic prayer such as the Lord's Prayer or the Glory Be. I ask God to come to me, and I name for God the topic about which I would like to pray.

3. I spend a few moments getting myself quiet. I might hum a religious song for a while. I stay with this quieting down as long as it feels right. Some days this will take up the entire prayer time—which is all right; sometimes getting quiet and receptive toward God is the most important part of prayer.

4. If I feel moved to do so, I pick up the object I've placed by my side. I read the Scripture passage. I look intently at the photograph. I hold my wedding ring in the palm of my hand. If I don't have any such object, then I close my eyes and place before me an image that moves me: the person I have strong feelings for, the city I'm being transferred to, the sin I hope to be freed of.

5. As best I can, I now let God take over and let whatever happens happen. My only job is to hold that object or image, to mull it over in my mind and heart. I avoid getting too analytical about it; I don't use this time for intellectual reasoning. Instead, I simply sit with this matter: I hold it not only in my hand or in my head but most especially in my heart. I allow this matter to move me to some deep emotion: joy, fear, contentment, anger, peace, longing, sorrow.

6. I sense that Jesus or God the Father is present with me in this matter. I imagine God being moved by this as well, and I begin to sense the way in which God is moved. I notice that the way my heart is feeling about the matter is moving in sync with the way God is feeling about it. Or I notice the opposite—that we seem to have different feelings about it. I listen quietly for anything God might want to say to me. I listen for anything my heart might be saying to God.

7. When I feel moved to do so, I gently pull out of the prayer. I pray the Lord's Prayer another time. Then I thank God for this moment, and I close with the sign of the cross.

My prayer life will go more smoothly if I have a consistent time and place, and rituals for starting and closing.

For example, I might pray in my overstuffed living-room chair every morning before the kids wake up or on a park bench in the middle of my evening jog. I might begin every prayer with a Glory Be or end it with a song of quiet praise. I might light a special candle, hold a sacred object, or cover myself with a blanket or prayer shawl. Each person will discover her own unique settings, and each will have to adjust those settings from time to time in order to keep her prayer life fresh and vibrant.

It is highly recommended that I work with a mentor or spiritual director who has been praying this way for a while.

I will need someone to speak to about my prayer as questions or problems arise. I might need advice if my prayer life becomes a little stale and boring, for example. Or I might want help discerning the topic of my prayer. I might need to speak aloud what I think is happening in my prayer before I can make sense of it. I might also need affirmation from my mentor from time to time.

Phase 2:
Gather Data

> Since [Ignatius] was an avid reader of books of worldly fiction, commonly called chivalrous romances, and since he was feeling quite well, he asked for some such books to pass the time. In that house, however, they found none of the type he was used to reading, and so they brought him The Life of Christ and a book on the lives of the saints in Spanish. By frequent reading of these books he grew somewhat fond of what he found written therein.
>
> AUTOBIOGRAPHY, 44–45

Phase 2 is straightforward and easy to understand. If by this point I have lots of options from which to choose (for example, I am leading a job search and have numerous applications before me), my mission statement will probably make it easy to toss out all but about two or three choices. This, then, is a good time to roll up my sleeves and do a bit of solid research. For each of my options, I should gather as much information as I possibly can. I will visit relevant people and places, I will Google one topic and then another. I will speak to experts. I will photocopy charts, photos, and executive summaries. I will ask questions, lots and lots of questions.

Again, my support network (mentors, companions, members of my church family) will be invaluable to me. If I am discerning a vocation to religious life, for instance, I will take the vocation brochures to my mentor and ask her what she thinks. I will invite my friend to visit a religious community with me. If I am discerning whether or not to remain in a difficult marriage, I will learn the church's teaching on marriage, divorce, and annulment. I will seek out the advice of good couples who have weathered marital storms and respected men and women who have had to exit their marriages. If I am discerning which college to attend, I will ask my favorite teachers for their opinions and will inquire of them what questions they would ask of each college.

What would my prayer be like at this stage? The next two phases will be the more crucial time of prayer. For now, I can tranquilly place my life in God's hands. I tell God, again, how much I want to do his will and how much I want to be available for the particular life, job, relationship, or commitment to which God has called me. I ask God to deepen my indifference. I return to my mission statement, prayerfully repeating it over and over again. I place the options before God and even place the brochure, the application, or a relevant photograph on my Bible as I pray, but I don't push too hard for an answer just yet. Instead, I brainstorm with God what might be the best questions to ask and the best avenues to explore.

Prayer Exercise E: Prayerful Brainstorming

Consider the following Bible story, in which God sends the prophet Samuel to choose the next king of Israel from among the sons of Jesse.

> [God said to Samuel,] "I will show you what you shall do; and you shall anoint for me the one whom I name to you." Samuel did what the LORD commanded, and came to Bethlehem. . . . When [the sons of Jesse] came, [Samuel] looked on Eliab and thought, "Surely the LORD's anointed is now before the LORD." But the LORD said to Samuel, "Do not look on his appearance or on the height of his stature, because I have rejected him; for the LORD does not see as mortals see, they look on the outward appearance, but the LORD looks on the heart." Then Jesse called Abinadab, and made him pass before Samuel. He said, "Neither has the LORD chosen this one." Then

Jesse made Shammah pass by. And he said, "Neither has the LORD chosen this one." Jesse made seven of his sons pass before Samuel, and Samuel said to Jesse, "The LORD has not chosen any of these." Samuel said to Jesse, "Are all your sons here?" And he said, "There remains yet the youngest, but he is keeping the sheep." And Samuel said to Jesse, "Send and bring him; for we will not sit down until he comes here." He sent and brought him in. Now he was ruddy, and had beautiful eyes, and was handsome. The LORD said, "Rise and anoint him; for this is the one." (1 Samuel 16:3–12)

So many times in life, we begin with the naive assumption that we have only options A and B. We choose one of these two without ever stopping to think that there might be an option C and D, and maybe even an option Q. Before going further in this decision-making process, then, we should spend several prayer times going over the situation again and again, thinking wild thoughts about crazy ways to respond. It just may be that there is some hidden, viable option—some ruddy David out in the field of your imagination—that will reveal itself in the midst of this holy brainstorming.

In your prayer, then, go back to the basic questions and ask them as though they have never been asked before.

- What's the problem or situation I'm dealing with here?
- What are *all* of the opportunities?
- Who are *all* of the people involved?
- What is option C? option D? option Q?

Do not leave this line of questioning until you have come up with a thousand new ideas, 90 percent of them extreme and unworkable. Then take that one workable solution you had not previously thought of and bring it to the decision-making process.

Hasty or Hesitant?

The earlier point about not pushing too hard for a quick answer opens up another important topic. It is in this phase of gathering data that I might want to reflect on the *timing* of the decision that I am to make. I may want to ask myself if I tend to be a hasty or a hesitant decision maker. The answer to that question could have important implications.

Important decisions are hard to make and involve an inner tension that begs to be resolved. I am tempted, then, to do one of two things with my decision. I may be tempted to jump too fast—to resolve the tension by making a quick (and rash) act and be done with it. Or I may be tempted not to jump at all—to pretend to be working on the decision, all the while hoping that it resolves itself. It may indeed resolve itself, but not necessarily in the way God wills.

Above all, trust in the slow work of God. We are quite naturally impatient in everything to reach the end without delay. We should like to skip the intermediate stages. We are impatient of being on the way to something unknown, something new. And yet, it is the law of all progress that it is made by passing through some stages of instability—and that it may take a very long time.

And so I think it is with you. Your ideas mature gradually—let them grow, let them shape themselves, without undue haste. Don't try to force them on, as though you could be today what time (that is to say, grace and circumstances acting on your own good will) will make of you tomorrow.

Only God could say what this new spirit gradually forming within you will be. Give Our Lord the benefit of believing that his hand is leading you. And accept the anxiety of feeling yourself in suspense and incomplete.

—Pierre Teilhard de Chardin, SJ

It's wise, then, to know what kind of a decision maker I am. Do I rush through decisions to get them over with, or do I wait too long to deal with them? The false spirit will take advantage accordingly. If I tend to rush things, then the false spirit will play on my impatience and panic to move me too quickly through the decision-making process. I will be convinced that the decision has to be made now, before it's too late. Fear or anticipation might move me to act before I've thoroughly discerned God's will.

It follows, then, that if I'm a hasty decision maker, I should commit myself to moving slowly through the process. I even determine *not* to decide before a certain deadline or benchmark. Doing so may keep me from listening to the false spirit, whispering in my ear, "You've got to act now! You can't wait any longer!"

If I am a hesitant decision maker, the false spirit may again use fear but this time to paralyze me. I will be convinced that I need more information before I can decide and that a bad decision will lead to terrible consequences. I may subconsciously avoid the consequences of making a decision by gathering data for an inordinate amount of time.

Perhaps a part of a hesitant person's problem is having to choose one great choice at the expense of the others. Generation Xers in particular seem to struggle with committing to one thing if it means having to say no to others. The writer Sylvia Plath presented a heartbreaking image of this paralysis in her book *The Bell Jar*:

> I saw my life branching out before me like the green fig tree in the story. From the tip of every branch, like a fat purple fig, a wonderful future beckoned and winked. One fig was a husband and a happy home and children, and another fig was a famous poet, and another fig was a brilliant professor. . . . I saw myself sitting in the crotch of this fig tree, starving to death, just because I couldn't make up my mind which of the figs I would choose. I wanted each and every one of them, but choosing one meant losing all the rest, and as I sat there, unable to decide, the figs began to wrinkle and go black, and one by one, they plopped to the ground at my feet.

If I am such a person, I may need to set a deadline for this phase of gathering data. I may need to push myself to move forward, even if I'm dissatisfied with my grasp of the necessary data. I do so because I know myself; I know that avoidance is a common defense mechanism for me and that I will never be satisfied that I have enough information.

It is possible, too, that I am too hasty at one phase of the discernment and too hesitant at another. As I proceed through the discernment, I may have to step back and examine the spirits that are influencing the timing of the process. At any given moment along the way, I may need to set a timeline for my decision in order to set the pace of one phase or another.

Hasty decision maker: Someone who tends to jump too quickly into a decision, someone who makes a decision without thoroughly discerning.	**Hesitant decision maker:** Someone who drags his or her feet in making a decision, usually because the decision requires an uncomfortable choice.

I'll need to adjust the timeline as my discernment proceeds; I should not become a slave to it. However, if I'm considering adjusting the timeline in the direction of my unhealthy tendency (my tendency is toward hastiness, and I consider shortening my timeline, or my tendency is toward procrastination, and I considering lengthening the timeline), then I should be slow to make such a change. I should seriously consider not doing so if my support network thinks it inadvisable.

The Reality of Deadlines

Like it or not, the situation might come with its own deadlines. Application deadlines, event dates, or corporate action plans may dictate the timeline of my decision. But even in these circumstances, some prayerful

	Hasty decision maker	Hesitant decision maker
Figure 6: How a Hasty or Hesitant Decision Maker Might Be Tempted To Act in Times of Desolation or False Consolation		
In desolation	Emotion: Panic Nagging thought: "Act now or it'll be too late!" Parable: Unwise builder and unwise general Luke 14:28–32	Emotion: Fear Nagging thought: "Hunker down!" Parable: Investor who buries money Matthew 25:14–30
In false consolation	Emotion: Euphoria Nagging thought: "More is better" Parable: Unwise virgins Matthew 25:1–13	Emotion: Self-satisfaction Nagging thought: "Good enough as it is." Parable: Man with storage bins Luke 12:15–21
Note: St. Ignatius cautions that I be particularly wary of a hasty decision maker in desolation (first quadrant).		

consideration could be made in terms of how I pace my discernment within the fixed time allotted me.

Often a person is pressured to decide something at the very moment that someone brings up the problem. Sometimes it's true: the decision needs to be made immediately. But at other times, the pressure to decide quickly is rooted in the *other* person's unhealthy anxieties. Despite the rhetoric of the person pressuring me, the decision really can wait an hour, a day, perhaps even a week or longer. If I do have a timeline for the decision, perhaps I could share it with this anxious person in the hopes of settling him down a bit.

Sometimes, though, I will have no choice. I will be forced to make a quicker decision than would be ideal. In those moments, I will fight for any time I can get (fifteen minutes, even). I will go through these phases as calmly and thoroughly as I can, and then will make the decision in peace, knowing that our God is a God of love and mercy and will always make good of my sincere efforts to serve him.

When I have exhausted every avenue of information, or when I have reached my self-imposed deadline for this phase, then I can gather up all the information and go into a sort of spiritual seclusion. That's when I step away from the experts and friends, from the Internet and the reference book. I move instead into my quiet place of prayer. If it is truly my decision to make and mine alone, then there must be a moment when I close off all but one resource: the God I find in my private prayer.

For instance, all through the process of writing this book, I am in touch with numerous resources. I am in regular dialogue with my publisher. I read books on the subject of discernment; I hand out copies of early drafts and get feedback from mentors and friends. But for each important decision that I must make, I eventually need to thank all these resources, step into my room, and close the door. I sit in my armchair, say a little prayer, and then God and I set to work. When I have come to this point in my information gathering, when all sides have had their say and every option has been thoroughly researched, it is then that I am ready for the next phase: to prayerfully dream the dreams.

Phase 3:
Dream the Dreams—
Tapping into Deep Desires

> While reading the life of our Lord and those of the saints, he used to pause and meditate, reasoning with himself: "What if I were to do what Saint Francis did, or to do what Saint Dominic did?" Thus in his thoughts he dwelt on many good deeds, always suggesting to himself great and difficult ones .... Throughout these thoughts he used to say to himself: "Saint Dominic did this, so I have to do it too. Saint Francis did this, so I have to do it too." These thoughts lasted a long time.
>
> *AUTOBIOGRAPHY*, 47

In chapter 6, I explored the necessity of being indifferent to every option before me. I saw what a blessed gift from God it is to receive indifference of the heart that allows me truly to desire any and all the options set before me. If I did not have this grace of indifference of the heart, then I should work on and pray for indifference of the will—acknowledging my inclination toward one or another option but choosing to stand on the foundation of deeper desires and thus choose that which gives God *greater* glory—the *Magis*, as St. Ignatius called it.

Magis: Dreaming of the greater glory of God. The desire to choose that which gives God more glory.

After learning of Ignatius's encouragement to be indifferent, we might mistakenly believe that Ignatius proposed giving up personal desires and preferences as obstacles to good discernment. Nothing could be further from the truth. Actually, Ignatius filled *The Spiritual Exercises* with exhortations to begin every prayer with "asking God for what I desire." He included "directives for finding more readily what one desires" and gave advice for the sad case "when someone making the Exercises fails to find what he or she desires." Why would a saint who elsewhere in his writings is so interested in penance and abnegation be preoccupied with desires?

Many spiritual writers of Ignatius's day spoke of desires as obstacles to God's will. A person was supposed to suppress his desires—to eliminate them whenever possible. But Ignatius held the radical notion that *God dwells within our desires*. Not only are desires not evil, but they are also one of God's primary instruments of communicating to us. God inflames the heart with holy desires and with attractions toward a life of greater divine praise and service. Unlike many of his religious contemporaries of the sixteenth century, Ignatius did not seek to quash desires but to tap into the deepest desires of the heart, trusting that it is God who has placed them there.

So then, at the very *beginning* of the process, while disposing myself to the gift of indifference, I try to set my preferences

> The soul is the place where God's desires and my desires intersect.

and inclinations aside in favor of desiring nothing more than the will of God. *Now*, at this phase in the process—*while grounded in indifference*—I can pick up again the desires of my heart. Doing so now, as an indifferent discerner, I can contemplate my desires without being a servant to them. Without indifference, the desires of my heart will manipulate my discernment, perhaps even without my noticing. But if I am indifferent—if I am ready to serve God in any capacity God wishes—then I can read those desires in the way a meteorologist reads his data-collecting instruments.

Desires, of course, do play a role in our sinful choices. But Ignatius would define sin as *disordered* desire. The problem is not that we have desires but that they are disordered—that is, out of balance or too heavily influencing our decisions. That is why we need to begin this entire process by tapping into the greatest, most universal desires of all: to praise, reverence, and serve God.

Some examples might help. A teenager wants badly to have sex with his girlfriend. Is this an evil desire? No, it is merely disordered. Why does he want to have sex? Because he craves oneness with another—he is wired for the experience of transcendent unity. A woman desires to "tell off" her husband. In what ways might the roots of this desire be holy? Perhaps she has been too passive all these years. Perhaps she only now loves herself and values herself enough to stick up for what she believes is right. Perhaps she desires to reverence God's creation (her very self) by asserting herself. These deeper desires are not evil; they are, in fact, *holy*. They come from God. If she could focus on these great desires beneath the desire to tell off her husband, then she will not sin.

We fall into sin when we are ignorant of the true, God-given desires *beneath* the apparent desires. We sin, not because we are in touch with our desires, but precisely because we are not in touch with them! This is one of Ignatius's most radical and most profound insights.

> The promise [of the incarnation] showed that their wildest dreams had simply not been wild enough.
>
> —MICHAEL CARD

How then do I tap into these great desires? I dream. I fanaticize about great and beautiful futures. *I let God dream in me,* and I sit in silent awe and wonder as these holy dreams come to life before the eyes and ears of my soul.

I dream. I start with option A and allow God to show me the marvelous and holy possibilities that could result from that option. I think crazy thoughts and mull over preposterous proposals. I have galactic visions of new worlds of possibilities opening up merely because I say yes to God's invitation to option A. I then start all over again and dream about option B, then about option C, and so on.

Concretely, how does this work? Let us say that I am a lawyer who has just been given an offer to relocate to a faraway city and join a more prestigious law firm. My immediate inclination might be to feel frightened of all the threatening unknowns: Will my family be happy in this new place? Will I like my new bosses? Will I find affordable housing? Will I be burning bridges with my current firm? All these are reasonable concerns and will have to be considered later (see chapter 8). But for now, I start off with dreams and desires.

I begin by asking the big questions: What is my purpose in life? To praise, reverence, and serve God. How am I uniquely called to do this? First, as a husband and father. Second, as a lawyer. As a husband and father, what are my dreams for my family? First, that we be healthy and safe. Second, that we be a family bonded with love and care for one another. Third, that our children might be not merely well-educated, but also well-formed in church and school. How might I make these goals come to life in option A, remaining here in my current job? I now dream great dreams of all that could happen in the life of our family if we remained here. How might I make these goals come to life in option B, moving to the new job and city? I now dream great dreams of all that could happen in the life of our family if we moved.

Now I move to my secondary vocation: the law profession. What are my great dreams for myself as a lawyer? What great desires led me to become a lawyer in the first place? Provided I've come to the heart of these dreams and desires, that is, to the holiest part of them, I now ask, How might I make these dreams and desires come true by remaining here? How might I do so by moving on?

Note the difference between the way most people normally discern and this radical way that Ignatius is proposing. Most lead with the wrong foot: they allow the tools of the false spirit to drive the bus: fear and anxiety *(What will happen?)*, ambition *(Here's my chance to rise!)*, pride *(It's a more prestigious law firm.)*, jealousy *(Finally, I'll leave my partners in the dust!)*, and so on. There will be time enough to deal with these negative realities (and since they are realities, we don't want to ignore them). But for now, I allow my great desires to drive the bus. I imagine the greatest potentialities—the best-case scenarios—for each option. For now, I dream of glorious possibilities.

Phase 4:
Ponder the Dreams—
Weighing Desolations and Consolations

There was this difference, however. When he thought of worldly matters, he found much delight; but after growing weary and dismissing them, he found that he was dry and unhappy. But when he thought of . . . imitating the saints in all the austerities they practiced, he not only found consolation in these thoughts, but even after they had left him he remained happy and joyful. He did not consider nor did he stop to examine this difference until one day his eyes were partially opened, and he began to wonder at this difference and to reflect upon it. From experience he knew that some thoughts left him sad while others made him happy, and little by little he came to perceive the different spirits that were moving him; one coming from the devil, the other coming from God.

AUTOBIOGRAPHY, 48

As I allow myself to dream crazy dreams, I then begin to ponder those dreams. As I daydream—or better, *praydream*—the possibilities of living out my great desires in each option, I try to note the difference in my heart as Ignatius did when comparing his dreams of chivalry with his dreams of religious life. I ask myself, *Which of these dreams leave me dry and sad, despite my best efforts to create a dream of great possibility? In which dreams have I found pleasure that lingers, even long after the dream ends?*

Which dreams leave me in consolation?

- Which of these dreams leave me filled with holy and wholesome desires?

- Which leave me with a sense of closeness to God?
- Which leave me filled with faith? with hope? with love?
- Which make me want to go out and proclaim them to the world and especially to my mentors and companions?
- Which leave me with a deep-down peace and tranquility? with a sense of rightness? with a fits-like-a-glove sort of feeling?

Which dreams leave me in desolation?

- Which leave me without faith? without hope? without love?
- Which leave me without a sense of God's closeness?
- Which leave me disquieted and agitated?
- Which leave me with no passion and no zeal? with a sense of boredom and tepidity? with no energy? feeling deflated?
- Which fill me with deep-down anxiety and fear?
- Which are the dreams I'm not very excited to talk about with my mentors or companions? Which are the ones that I avoid mentioning to them?

Pondering these questions while dreaming of my future is the very heart of Ignatian discernment. This moment in my discernment is the very essence of Ignatius's discovery of the discernment of spirits. It is the sun around which orbit all the other insights of Ignatian discernment.

The love that moves and causes one to choose must descend from above, that is, from the love of God, so that before one chooses he should perceive that the greater or less attachment for the object of his choice is solely because of His Creator and Lord.

—SE, P. 76

As I dream these praydreams, I pay particular attention to the fluctuating moments of peace versus disquiet, and of impassioned energy versus deflatedness.

Peace versus Disquiet

[T]he action of the good angel is delicate, gentle, delightful. It may be compared to a drop of water penetrating a sponge.

—SE, RULES FOR DISCERNMENT OF SPIRITS, SECOND WEEK, #7

Ignatius says that when a well-intentioned, prayerful person is in consolation, God's will comes "sweetly, lightly, gently, as a drop of water that enters a sponge." These descriptors are among the most important telltale signs of God's will in the particular option I am considering. When I ponder my praydreams, which of the options left me feeling this way? Which leave me with a sense of deep-down peace? Note that I am searching for the *deep-down* peace, as opposed to simply feeling comfortable with the option. It may well be that God's will lies in the most frightening option (for example, leaving my comfortable job in order to enter religious life, firing an unfit employee instead of ignoring the problem, or choosing an unpopular course of action). I may therefore feel fearful when I praydream this scenario, and yet deeper down there is a sense that this is the proper way to go and that God's abiding presence will sustain me through the unpleasant fallout. It is this "deeper-down" peace that I am looking for.

I am also looking for its opposite—for deep-down agitation. Again, one particular option may look good on paper and make me feel comfortable on the surface of my emotions. This option may smooth things over, sidestep conflict, or avoid unpleasant or awkward situations (for example, upholding the status quo, remaining in current status, not making waves at the office, making only complimentary remarks). But despite the fact that this option is clearly the path of least resistance, deeper down there is agitation within me. There is something that isn't quite settled in my spirit as I imagine myself moving forward in this direction. This negative indicator of sensing agitation is as important as the positive indicator of sensing deep-down peace.

Just a few years into my tenure as a teacher and pastoral minister at Strake Jesuit School in Houston, I received a phone call from one of my superiors asking if I felt ready to leave Houston and move on to the next assignment. It was the call I knew was coming yet dreaded, nonetheless. My years in this particular ministry had been among the best of my life. My relationship with the students was strong, healthy, and mutually nourishing. I loved teaching more with each passing year. I found my priesthood thriving as I ministered to the wider community. I had close friendships and a loving community of brother Jesuits with whom I lived. Why on earth would I want to leave this grace-filled moment and place?

Praydreaming over staying in Houston several more years left me feeling comfortable, safe, and loved. But *deeper down*, despite my hesitance to lose this blessed life, I felt an itch—a disquiet. Despite my fears of the unknown, I felt a pull to say yes to whatever it was God had in store for me next. When I praydreamed about leaving Houston and taking on this or that assignment in this or that city, I felt the pang of saying good-bye to a place I called home. I felt the discomfort of moving from something I had learned to do well to moving to work I knew nothing about. I felt nervous about being in a new place with no friends and no familiar surroundings. But *deeper down*, there was a sense of peace and rightness. Deeper down, I felt a stronger presence of the creative energy of the Creator working with, in, and through me.

Owing to these deeper dynamics of peace and agitation, I was able to answer my superiors, "Yes, I'm ready to leave."

Inflamed Energy versus Deflatedness

I call it consolation when . . . [the soul] is inflamed with love of its Creator and Lord. . . .

I call it desolation . . . when the soul is wholly slothful, tepid, sad, and separated, as it were, from its Creator and Lord.

—SE, RULES FOR DISCERNMENT OF SPIRITS, FIRST WEEK, #3 AND #4

Earlier, when discussing Ignatian indifference, I mentioned that my provincial superior once asked me to pray about three or four different possibilities for my future. One of the possibilities was to become vocation director for the Jesuits in my province. This was not a surprise to me, because my friends frequently remarked on how much I enjoyed working with interested candidates and since I, too, over the years, had often dreamed of having this job. However, when I praydreamed this work for myself at this particular moment in my life, I was surprised by what I felt and didn't feel. Here is an excerpt from the letter I sent in reply:

> [In regard to the position of vocation director], truthfully, I've always hoped to get into this type of work. I do love working with associates and I think I'm pretty good at it. So, I would be happy to be the next vocation director. Interestingly, though, over the past few weeks of praying about it, I haven't felt the great desires to do this work that I have felt in the past. I'm not exactly sure why that is the case.

The questions that I asked myself in this discernment was, *Where is the energy? Where is the passionate desire?* In this particular case, while I had felt passionate desire for vocation work in the past, I presently was not sensing that same energy. When I prayed over one or two of the other possibilities, a crackle of electricity ran through me. When I prayed over the vocation-director job, despite its seeming the perfect fit for my skill set and personality, I felt less energy. I could envision myself doing the work and even enjoying it, but I didn't feel "the baby leap in my womb for joy," as Elizabeth described her recognition of God's presence in her pregnant cousin, Mary. This leaping prenatal John the Baptist is a good metaphor for the kind of reaction my soul has when coming in contact with the presence of God in some pregnant possibility of my future—my soul leaps with joy and excitement.

This, then, is the pinnacle of my discernment. If I have faithfully journeyed through my discernment process, there will come a moment when peace and the life-giving energy of pregnant possibility will accompany one of these options. There will be a moment at this point in my discernment when I sense a *transcendent* peace and tranquility and an undeniable *yes* that pulses through my veins every time I imagine myself going with one particular option over the others. All the other options will begin to fade and, on their own, will become ever distant in the horizon of my praydreams.

A Special Case:
"When the Soul Is Not Acted on by Various Spirits"

Sometimes, in a life of discernment, there is no strong sense of the spirits within—when dreaming over the various possibilities, the person does not sense a deep-down peace or deep-down agitation, neither impassioned energy nor deflated tepidity. It's not that she has negative feelings but rather that she doesn't have strong feelings at all. Since the true and false interior movements are the bread and butter of Ignatian discernment, what does a person do when she senses the presence of neither?

In such circumstances, Ignatius says that we must rely on our natural senses of reason and judgment. We must weigh the facts through intellectual investigation and note which option seems most appropriate and reasonable given the strengths and weaknesses of each option, the opportunities and threats of each situation, and the skills and limitations in our areas of competency. True to form, Ignatius has insightful and pragmatic suggestions as to how we might consider the options before us.

I can apply the general ideas in my mission statement to the present circumstances. Ignatius says, "I must consider only the end for which I am created, that is, for the praise of God our Lord and for the salvation of my soul. Hence, whatever I choose must help me to this end for which I am created" (SE, p. 71). In my prayer, I return to the mission statement I've written at the beginning of the discernment process. I start with the most basic statements and move to the more particular, then push the convictions further to define my mission in this particular circumstance.

For example, let us again consider the case of a young woman choosing a college destination. Let's say that in setting down her mission statement, this young woman was struck by her call to serve the poor in some concrete fashion. Pushing further this call to service, she found herself thanking God for her high school community-service work in the emergency room of the local hospital. Upon reflection, she began to wonder if she weren't called to this work on a more permanent basis: *Am I to be a doctor or a nurse?*

Now, at this step, she takes up this question again. She's not at all sure that she's called to the medical field, but she does feel called to explore that option, and she definitely feels called to serve the community in the way she served at the hospital. While reflecting on this, she recalls how one of her college options has a community-service component built into the curriculum. She also remembers that this same school has an excellent premed program. One of the other schools is closer to home, and more of her friends would be attending there. But her mission statement makes her more attracted to the school that more easily allows her to serve in the way she has recently felt called.

Ignatius insisted throughout his writing that we keep as our objective the end for which we were created. It would be wise, then, to begin each of my prayer times in this phase of discernment by reading my mission statement, my first principle and foundation. Doing so will set the tone for each of the other ways I pray over this decision.

Ignatius advises me to contemplate the decision by prayerfully making a list of pros and cons.

> [I ought] to weigh the matter [option A] by reckoning the number of advantages and benefits that would accrue to me if I had the proposed office or benefice solely for the praise of God our Lord and the salvation of my soul. On the other hand, I should weigh the disadvantages and dangers there might be in having it. I will do the same with the second alternative [option B], that is, weigh the advantages and benefits as well as the disadvantages and danger of not having it.

After I have gone over and pondered in this way every aspect of the matter in question, I will consider which alternative appears more reasonable. Then I must come to a decision in the matter under deliberation because of weightier motives presented to my reason, and not because of any sensual inclinations.

—SE, P. 76

In considering a vocation to religious life, for example, I could list in my journal all the wonderful things about being a religious brother or priest. I could then list the downsides of this life choice. Next, I could list all the things I would love about being a husband, a father, a career man. Finally, I could list the downsides of this life choice. When I am finished making these four lists, I could pray over each item, weighing it in terms of importance to me. Perhaps in the process of considering the weightier advantages and disadvantages, it will become clearer which way I should move.

I can imagine myself as a mentor to someone younger or less experienced.

I should represent to myself a man whom I have never seen or known, and whom I would like to see practice all perfection. Then I should consider what I would tell him to do and choose for the greater glory of God our Lord and the greater perfection of his soul. I will do the same, and keep the rule I propose to others.

—SE, P. 77

Perhaps I could put before my mind my little brother, or a younger employee at work, or the kid behind the coffee-shop counter. I play an imaginative scene in my head in which this younger person is trying to make the decision that I'm currently discerning. In my prayerful imagination, I listen to the advice I give, the questions I ask, the encouragements and discouragements I speak. When the scene is over, I write in my journal the things I learned from the exercise. I try to follow the advice I would have given the person who came to me in this imagined situation.

Another Ignatian way would be to imagine myself as a very old person near the end of my life or perhaps just after I have died.

> [I ought] to consider what procedure and norm of action I would wish to have followed in making the present choice if I were at the moment of death. I will guide myself by this and make my decision entirely in conformity with it.
>
> Let me picture and consider myself as standing in the presence of my judge on the last day, and reflect what decision in the present matter I would then wish to have made. I will choose now the rule of life that I would then wish to have observed, that on the day of judgment I may be filled with happiness and joy.
>
> —SE, P. 77

I imagine looking back over the scenes of my life, starting with my young life and proceeding to the present. I imagine looking back on my choice of option A. Am I proud and happy to have made this choice, or am I embarrassed and desiring to move past this scene? I do the same with the other options. I then imagine myself as having died and looking back from the afterlife at choosing option A. How do I feel as I look back on this? Then I move to option B, and so on.

Beyond Ignatius's insights, there are still more ways that I could pray over these options.

- I could find relevant Scripture passages on which to read and reflect. If I am discerning about marriage for example, I could look up every passage in which Jesus speaks on the subject. I could reflect on the good and bad marriages/families of the Bible.

- I could do stream-of-consciousness journaling. That is, I put pen to paper at the beginning of my prayer time and just start writing. I don't think about what I'll write next, I just write and write without stopping. I don't worry about grammar, style, or cohesiveness; I write the first things that pop into my head. Sometimes by doing this, I'll pull some insight about myself out of my unconscious. In prayerfully rereading my writing, I might be shocked by the results!

> It's possible to pull tips on mental discerning from the business world. A popular model in the business world is the S.W.O.T. analysis. In looking at the options for the company, the execs ask, "What are the strengths, weaknesses, opportunities, and threats involved in this option?
>
> I could make S.W.O.T. a prayerful activity by journaling these questions during my prayer time and by starting off and ending the prayer time with meditating over my Mission Statement.

All these mental deliberations can be fruitful in any discernment process, but they are particularly helpful in the special case of not sensing any interior movement as I praydream over the various options. The hope is that these mental exercises will jump-start my passions and get the various spirits moving in my heart.

Figure 7: Mental Deliberations
1. I work from my mission statement.
2. I weigh the pros and cons.
3. I consider the strengths, weaknesses, opportunities, and threats.
4. I ask, How would I mentor someone in this situation?
5. I ask, At the end of life, what do I want to look back upon?
6. I meditate over relevant Scripture passages.
7. I do stream-of-consciousness journaling.

Another Special Case: "Without Being Able to Doubt"

Ignatius mentions that there may be times when God moves the soul in an extraordinary way and provides such passion and clarity that there can be no doubt about the path that I should follow.

> God our Lord so moves and attracts the will that a devout soul without hesitation, or the possibility of hesitation, follows what has been manifested to it. St. Paul and St. Matthew acted thus in following Christ our Lord.
>
> —SE, P. 74

Consider the story of how I ended up choosing to become a Jesuit priest instead of a diocesan priest.

How I Ended Up a Jesuit

I wanted to be a priest almost since before I can remember. But because I was really familiar with only one of the many types of priesthood, the diocesan priesthood, I presumed that this was the type of priest I would be. Still, there was always a nagging feeling in me that maybe I should be some other type of priest, like a Franciscan, a Dominican, or a Benedictine. I remember telling my spiritual director, a diocesan priest himself, about my troubles. "What if God is calling me to be something crazy like a Tibetan monk or something? How the heck would I know?"

My wise director said, "Look, you've come this far with the diocesan group, and you feel happy with them don't you?"

"Yes, very much."

"Well," he said, "Tell God that this is the route you think he wants you to go. Tell him that if he wants you to change course, he's got to knock you off your horse on the way to Damascus. Otherwise, you'll presume that this route is the will of God." Mike was referring to St. Paul, who, before he became Christian, was on his way to Damascus to *arrest* Christians when Jesus Christ knocked him to the ground and told him to become one. So, I went to prayer and told God that he would have to knock me off my horse if he wanted me to do something different with my life. This set my heart at ease.

This was my last year of high school. On January 29, during civics class, my friend Mitchell mentioned in passing that a former teacher of ours said that I should become a Jesuit. Mitchell and I laughed at that, but I thought little more about it. I was already halfway through my application process for the diocesan seminary and was content with this path. During English class, my classmates and I were in the library making note cards for our research papers when the strangest thing happened: I was suddenly overwhelmed with excitement over the prospect of becoming a Jesuit. This was extraordinary, given that (a) all of this was happening in a public school; (b) I wasn't, at that moment, in a state of prayer; and (c) I hardly knew what a Jesuit was! Though no exterior vision or miraculous event had occurred, I sensed that a tectonic shift had just rocked my whole world. I looked up from my note card and said to my friend Tiffany, "What the heck am I supposed to do with my life?" Knowing nothing of what had just happened, Tiffany laughed; took a blank note card; and wrote my name, the date, and "Diagnosis: Senioritis;" and handed the card to me. I folded the card and carefully placed it inside my wallet. I wanted to keep it because I knew that I would always want to remember this precise moment. This card is framed now and sits on my bookshelf.

Later that day, I went directly to my spiritual director and said, "Do you remember when you told me to tell God to knock me off my horse if he wants me to do something else? Well, I think I've just got knocked off my horse!"

Days later, being completely unable to shake this obsession with a group I knew practically nothing about, I took my spiritual director's advice and called the nearest Jesuit community. When Father Madden answered the phone, I asked, "May I speak to a Jesuit, please? Anyone will do." A few days later I met with him. A few weeks later, I applied to the Jesuits, and a few months later, I was in the novitiate. I have never looked back.

This story does *not* reflect the normal pattern of vocation discernment, and I would not recommend that a person wait for such a moment before saying yes to whatever he or she feels called to. However, I do believe that this extraordinary moment was from God and that God, for his own reasons, wanted me to skip the ordinarily necessary phases and move right to the near end of the discernment process. Ignatius says of these rare experiences that one is "without being able to doubt," and that is exactly how I felt. In all the discernments I've made since, I cannot recall ever having such a moment of absolute clarity.

It is possible, then, that you the reader will be blessed with such a moment. There may come in an instant the unwavering certainty of what you are called to do. You should note, however, that in my twenty years since entering the Jesuits, I have rarely seen such a thing happen and I have often witnessed such a *perceived* moment turning out to be untrue. I have seen young men have a moment that they would describe much like mine, only to never end up in the Jesuits or to enter and leave shortly afterwards. This cautionary note warns that even these extraordinary moments must be tested. Even in my particular case, when it seemed impossible to entertain any doubt, still I went immediately to my spiritual director; I got advice from my wise and loving parents. I went through a rigorous application process with the Jesuits, and even after entering, I went through the normal two-year discernment period before taking any vows. I did not take vows as a Jesuit on the day this flash of knowing occurred, but only after two and a half years of thorough testing, deliberation, and discernment.

To use another example, as a priest preparing couples for marriage, I love to ask for the story of how they fell in love and how they decided to get married. It's not unusual for one or both of them to laugh and say, "I didn't like him [or her] at all at first!" But other times, one or both will say, "I knew that he [or she] was 'the one' from the moment I laid eyes on him [or her]." I feel a sort of kinship with such a person because this love-at-first-sight experience brings me back to my own vocational flash of transcendent certainty. However, just as mine was tested, so does every couple need to test their vocational discernment through speaking with their elders, doing marriage preparation, relating as an engaged couple for a while, and so on.

> After this [Jesus] went out and saw a tax collector named Levi, sitting at the tax booth; and he said to him, "Follow me." And he got up, left everything, and followed him.
>
> —LUKE 5:27-28

So then, even though Ignatius says that a person is unable to doubt in that moment, given our psyche's ability to mislead us, we should put in place a thorough and rigorous testing of the experience before making any long-term commitments to it. We should heed Ignatius's warning for a person who "is going on in consolation and in great fervor," that the person should not be "inconsiderate or hasty in making any promise or vow" (*SE*, Annotation 14).

Coming to a Decision

The special case of having no detectable interior movements is an uncommon experience; the special case of having an unmistakable attraction to one option is an even rarer occurrence. Most of the time, we will discern in the usual way of pondering the praydreams and comparing their accompanying inner movements to the characteristics of desolation and consolation. Like Ignatius in his convalescent pondering, once we've discovered the source of our attractions, dreams, desires, hesitations, and repulsions, then we'll begin to sense where the will of God is leading us.

Often, after many hours of prayerful deliberation, there will be a moment when a person just knows. It will feel not as though I am *making* a decision, but rather as though I am *acknowledging* a decision that my heart has already made. I'll recognize this auspicious moment by the way one option over the others leads to praydreams that are maybe not as idealistic or beautiful as when I first began to dream them but are somehow more realistic and right. These dreams will fit like a glove. All the other options—though perhaps more beautiful, more comfortable, or safer—will drift farther from my soul's watchful eye and will begin to fade into the horizon. Though I may not be able to put my finger on it, there will be something not quite right about those dreams; they will have a tinny ring to them which seems not to resonate with the rhythm of creation. It is then that I have come to my tentative decision.

8

After Deciding:
Tentative Decisions,
Confirmation,
and Final Decisions

After such a choice or decision, the one who has made it must turn with great diligence to prayer in the presence of God our Lord, and offer Him his choice that the Divine Majesty may deign to accept and confirm it if it is for His greater service and praise.

—SE, P. 76

S t. Ignatius has little to say about the present topic. This one sentence in the epigraph is the only instruction he provides in the *Spiritual Exercises*. And yet Jesuits and Ignatian scholars throughout the centuries have believed strongly that this penultimate act is a crucial part of the Ignatian tradition. They have surmised this based on observations of how Ignatius himself made decisions (as presented in his personal diary) and on their own life experience. Nonetheless, since Ignatius gives us so little practical instruction on the topic, we must rely heavily on conjecture. We must make educated guesses as to the details of this last moment of discernment.

Ignatius says that *after* the decision has been made, I am to *"offer"* God our Lord the decision so that God *"may . . . accept and confirm it if* it is for His greater service . . ."* (emphases mine). The implications of these few words are strong: *After* the decision, I *offer* it to God, who *may (or may not)* confirm it. If it is not conducive to God's greater (Magis) service, then God presumably will not confirm the offering of the tentative decision. Clearly, then, though I have made a thorough and well-reflected decision, I am not quite finished with Ignatian discernment. Ignatius knows what a tricky process discernment can be, and he provides one last opportunity for God to throw me off my horse if I'm not quite going in the right direction.

But how do I prayerfully offer the decision? How might God receive and confirm it? When can I be sure enough of that confirmation to move into making the final decision? In this chapter we will explore these questions and more.

Offering My Tentative Decision

After thoroughly discerning the matter at hand and after coming to a place where I feel that I know which option I should choose, I am ready to make a tentative decision, to offer that decision to God, and to await God's confirmation. If time and circumstances permit, I make some sort of interior pilgrimage. I set aside a special period in which to offer my tentative decision. I make a nine-day novena; I spend a Saturday hiking in the woods; I attend daily Mass for a time; I do an afternoon of quiet reflection at a monastery; or I make a retreat at a retreat house.

Once I have set aside the time and place, how do I prayerfully offer my decision? Here are a few suggestions.

- In my prayer I find some ritual by which to offer this decision to God. I can prayerfully imagine myself kneeling before God's altar. I imagine myself holding this decision in my hands and then placing it on the altar. I say to God, "I have come to believe that this is what you want me to do. Please let me know, in one form or another, whether or not I am correct—whether or not this is indeed the *Magis*, the greater glory of you. If this is not your will, please prevent me from moving forward."

- Remember when, at the advice of my spiritual director, I told God to knock me off my horse on the way to Damascus? At this stage in the discernment process, I can say the same to God. I can say, "Look, God, I'm not positive this is what you want, but it's my best guess as to your will. Please stop me if it isn't your will. Please knock me off my horse."

- In my prayer, I imagine myself eliminating all the other options. I think of all the praydreams I've had of these other options, and I shut them down one by one. I imagine what it would be like in real life to say no to each of these other options. If I am a high school senior, I imagine myself throwing away all the brochures of the other colleges and telling my family and friends that I'm not going to those places. If I have decided not to take the job in the other city, I imagine calling the person who made the offer to say, "No, thank you."

- In my prayer, I continue to praydream about living out the chosen option. Earlier, in the stage of dreaming the dreams, I praydreamed the "great desires" within this option—the best-case scenario of this option. Now, I praydream this option more realistically. I imagine the problems that may arise, the resistance in others that I might have to face, the difficulty of making this choice work. I imagine having to stick to the decision as my enthusiasm wanes over time. I imagine the long-term consequences of this decision.

Note that at this moment, I do all of this offering up through my *prayerful imagination*, not in my concrete life. It is not quite time to actually make the pledge, to say the no-thank-yous, or to start working through the problems. Right now, it is a purely interior activity.

A Hilarious Scriptural Example of Dis-confirmation!

There is another "knock you off your horse" kind of dis-confirmation story in the Bible, and it's a very funny one. It is the story of Balaam's ass, found in Numbers 22.

The Israelites were battling a variety of tribes to acquire the Promised Land and were presently battling the Moabites. Balak, the leader of the Moabites, bribed a wizard named Balaam to go over and curse the Israelites for him. Balaam was supposedly a seer and yet, as the story reveals, could not see a mighty sword-wielding angel that is in clear sight of his goofy donkey! The talking donkey (who is strikingly similar to the donkey in the *Shrek* movies), is much maligned for obeying the angel.

We take up the story where Balaam is on his way to curse the Israelites:

> God's anger was kindled because [Balaam] was going, and the angel of the LORD took his stand in the road as his adversary. Now he was riding on the donkey, and his two servants were with him. The donkey saw the angel of the LORD standing in the road, with a drawn sword in his hand; so the donkey turned off the road, and went into the field; and Balaam struck the donkey, to turn it back onto the road. Then the angel of the LORD stood in a narrow path between the vineyards, with a wall on either side. When the donkey saw the angel of the LORD, it scraped against the wall, and scraped Balaam's foot against the wall; so he struck it again. Then the angel of the LORD went ahead, and stood in a narrow place, where there was no way to turn either to the right or to the left. When the donkey saw the angel of the LORD, it lay down under Balaam; and Balaam's anger was kindled, and he struck the donkey with his staff. Then the LORD opened the mouth of the donkey, and it said to Balaam, "What have I done to you, that you have struck me these three times?" Balaam said to the donkey, "Because you have made a fool of me! I wish I had a sword in my hand! I would kill you right now!" But the donkey said to Balaam, "Am I not your donkey, which you have ridden all your life to this day? Have I been in the habit of treating you this way?" And he said, "No."

Then the LORD opened the eyes of Balaam, and he saw the angel of the LORD standing in the road, with his drawn sword in his hand; and he bowed down, falling on his face. The angel of the LORD said to him, "Why have you struck your donkey these three times? I have come out as an adversary, because your way is perverse before me. The donkey saw me, and turned away from me these three times. If it had not turned away from me, surely just now I would have killed you and let it live." Then Balaam said to the angel of the LORD, "I have sinned, for I did not know that you were standing in the road to oppose me. Now therefore, if it is displeasing to you, I will return home."

—NUMBERS 22:22–34

Seeking Confirmation

Note that the prayer activities of offering up are actually more forms of praydreaming. Now, instead of praydreaming various options, I praydream making my choice and living with the consequences of that choice. This entire phase of postdiscernment, then, is a form of prayerful lab testing. It is a way of metaphorically building a computer model of myself and my choice and pressing "play" to see what happens.

If offering the choice to God is a form of revisiting the phase "dream the dreams," then seeking confirmation is a form of repondering the dreams. So, just as I observed the inner movements within me as I dreamed the dreams earlier, I now observe the inner movements as I praydream these new dreams of pledging myself to the choice, eliminating the other choices, and of realistically dealing with the fallout of my choice. And I am looking for the same telltale characteristics that I looked for in the "ponder the dreams" stage: I am observing whether, dreaming through consequences of this choice, I sense the false spirit or the true spirit within me. Do these postdiscernment dreams bear the characteristics of consolation or of desolation? Figure B provides a helpful chart to determine this.

Rarely will every one of the items of the chart match perfectly with the interior movements. There may be times, for example, when I'm called to move away from some of the people who love me and support me. There may be other times when I need to make a radical choice that will be unpopular among my loved ones. However, generally speaking, the more the movements within me align with the sentiments of the consolation side of this chart, the more likely it is that I am receiving confirmation of that choice.

If this interior lab test is going well and I feel as though I am, in fact, receiving inner confirmation, and if time and circumstances permit, I could now try out my tentative decision exteriorly and seek exterior confirmation. For example:

- I am a lawyer and have tentatively decided to strike out on my own. I begin searching for office space and gathering the paperwork necessary to incorporate the new firm. My husband and I begin to make plans to adjust our lives to this decision.
- I have tentatively decided to stay with my girlfriend rather than join the seminary. I inform the vocation director and begin to meet with him less often. I begin instead to spend more quality time with my girlfriend and perhaps invite her home to meet my parents.
- I have tentatively decided to attend a distant university instead of the college in my hometown. I increase my correspondence with people I know there and I inform my best friend that I probably won't be rooming with her after all.

I have begun to live *as if* my permanent decision were made. While not yet burning any bridges, I have gently backed away from the other options and have moved toward the option I've temporarily chosen. As I do so, I go back to Figure B to seek signs of confirmation from God. In the example of the lawyer: How does it feel to drive around town looking at office space for my new firm? In the example of the young man inclined to grow closer to his girlfriend: Do I miss hanging out at the seminary? Does spending more time with my girlfriend bring me greater joy? peace? creative energy? And in the example of the college-bound student: With friends and family, what are the words I choose to describe my feelings about this other university? How does it feel to complete the paperwork for courses and for dorm preferences?

Ignatius boldly trusts a praying person's deep desires. So, as I move deeper into one choice and away from others, are my deep desires consistently in favor of this change? (Remember that we're talking here about *deep* desires. Even if this option *is* God's will, there will always be more superficial attractions to the other options.) Do I sense joyful anticipation or at least tranquil acceptance as I consider living with the consequences of this decision? Or, is there instead a deep sense of dread?

God's confirmation is not the same as others' affirmation.

Note that in seeking this exterior confirmation, I'm not neces-

> A voice cries out:
> "In the wilderness prepare the way of the LORD,
>   make straight in the desert a highway for our God.
> Every valley shall be lifted up,
>   and every mountain and hill be made low;
> the uneven ground shall become level,
>   and the rough places a plain.
> Then the glory of the LORD shall be revealed.
>
> —ISAIAH 40:3–5

sarily looking for affirmation from everyone. If I am an executive in a company or the pastor of a parish, for example, I will often be called to make unpopular decisions. So even on this exterior level, I am interested more in my inner spirit's reaction to the exterior data. "Is there *still* peace and creative energy within me even through the disparaging reactions of some people?" Likewise, in the case of disconfirmation, the opposite can be true: "Everyone seems so happy for me, and yet there is something bothering me deep within."

Another way to seek confirmation is to notice how easily or how laboriously the doors open as I move toward the option I've tentatively chosen. This is what Ignatius meant by tranquility. Usually, if it is of God, I won't have to *force* my way in—I won't have to shove the doors open. God typically smooths the path and removes the obstacles when I am stepping in the right direction. Ignatius says that confirmation will be "easing and taking away all obstacles, so that the person may go forward in doing good." If, however, I have to push my way into a new situation, to painstakingly convince wise and loving people despite their own

Figure 8: Signs of Confirmation or Disconfirmation	
As I praydream the consequences of having made my decision, I . . .	
• feel a little nervous, but deep down, I am at peace.	• feel fearful, anxious, or disquiet deep down.
• do not have all the answers, but I feel confident that God will lead me step by step. Despite my lack of certainty, I feel as though I am walking in the light.	• am agitated and confused. I am fretful about the future. I'm groping in the dark.
• feel God very near to me.	• do not feel God's presence.
• am stirred by great desires to work, to create, to act, to move. I am stirred toward acts of faith, hope, and love.	• feel paralyzed. I feel tepid, bored, slothful, lazy. I feel unattracted to faith, hope, and love.
• am stirred to action which ultimately if not immediately leads to lasting unity and reconciliation with the good aspects and people in my life.	• am stirred to inaction or to action that severs ties and burns bridges with good things and people in my life.
• am moved to spend more time with the ones I love and with prayer, church, and healthy behaviors. I am unattracted to bad influences in my life.	• am moved to neglect healthy well-established relationships and to neglect prayer, church, and healthy behaviors. I am attracted to bad influences in my life.
• see good fruits when I prayerfully ask myself, "Where will this lead?" The fruits are congruent with my principle and foundation.	• see bad fruits when I prayerfully ask myself, "Where will this lead?" The fruits are incongruent with my principle and foundation.
• feel as if I'm moving *toward* something good, like it's the natural evolution of the way God has been leading me for a while. If feels as if I'm saying yes to an invitation. It is congruent with past good decisions of my life.	• feel as if I'm moving *away* from something, like I'm breaking away from that which has healthily nourished me all along. It feels as if I'm fleeing something that frightens me. It is incongruent with past good decisions of my life or resembles past bad decisions.

Figure 8: Signs of Confirmation or Disconfirmation As I praydream the consequences of having made my decision, I . . . *continued*	
• look forward to talking about it with my support network. There is consensus of views within my support network.	• want to keep it a secret, especially from my support network. There is divergence of views within my support network.
• am stirred to act boldly, but in a measured fashion. I can do it now, but I don't have to. I'm indifferent to the timing of the act.	• am stirred to do something that wise people in my life think is reckless or rash. I must do it now although wise people are telling me there is no hurry.
• feel as if the other options, on their own, are moving to the background of my imagination.	• feel as if one or more of the other options keep nagging at me. They won't go away.

inclinations, to get authorities to bend the rules, to break commitments I've already made, then these are signs that I may not be receiving the confirmation that I seek.

Think of a sponge and a rock.

Ignatius describes the phenomenon this way: for the person who is gradually maturing in relationship with God, God's will comes as water falling on a sponge: time and circumstance seem to soak it up. If my decision is not of God's will, the steps I take in acting out this decision will be like the ocean crashing against a craggy shore: there is no absorption, no easy marriage between the new decision and my present life. There is instead conflict, incongruity, and unease.

There may, in fact, be occasions when the tentative decision I make wreaks havoc in the exterior world. For example, let us say that I am a successful businessman who has properly and thoroughly decided to enter a monastery. As I begin to enact this decision, there may well be a great deal of opposition. My boss may offer me more money. My siblings might try to talk me out of it. I may have trouble selling my house and getting rid of my possessions. These stumbling blocks *may or may not* be signs of disconfirmation.

Likewise, there may be occasions when, exteriorly, everything falls into place, but interiorly, there is no confirmation. For example, it is not unusual for a seminarian to properly discern to leave the seminary, despite the fact that, on the exterior, he seems to be a perfect fit. How, then, can I tell if I have confirmation or disconfirmation?

I return to the characteristics of desolation and confirmation. For example, in the case of the businessman-turned-monk, throughout all this havoc, is there an interior peace? Despite the fact that I *should* be discouraged by the exterior obstacles I've encountered, does there remain in me a sense of the "rightness" of this decision? In the case of the seminarian who seems a perfect fit, is there a deep-down disquiet, despite the fact that I am getting along quite well in the seminary? Throughout my happy engagement to be married, do I find myself constantly dogged by strong, deep-down desires to become a priest?

In the end, then, what matters is not so much what happens in the exterior but what interior movements are stirred in the midst of these exterior circumstances.

What If There Is No Confirmation?

What if my tentative decision is not confirmed? With the help of my mentors and companions, I will discern what to do next.

- If time and circumstance allow it, I may decide to put off the decision for now. I may need to back away from the whole process for a while and come back to it later with a fresh spirit.
- I may interiorly try out one of the other options, praydreaming the consequences of this alternative choice.
- I may decide to begin the whole process anew—to start from the very beginning by praying for indifference, setting down my first principle and foundation, getting quiet, dreaming the dreams, and so on.
- If circumstances force me to make a choice now and I am not experiencing any clear interior movement toward one option over another, then, according to Ignatius, I will have to rely on my reasoning skills to make the decision. I go back to the section titled "A Special Case: 'When the soul is not acted on by various spirits'" (see page 177).

After a long and thorough discernment process, receiving no confirmation may be discouraging and frustrating. *Where have I gone wrong? Was all that discernment misguided? Why won't God just tell me what he wants?* This could be a painful moment in my discernment process. If it is, then I need to acknowledge my frustration and take it to prayer. As best I can, I must be patient with the process, with myself, and with God.

Although my discouragement or frustration may tempt me to think that I've done a poor job at discerning, that may not be the case at all. I may well have done everything correctly and still arrive at the point of disconfirmation. Why would God allow this? Often in the spiritual life,

God leads me toward a particular calling to receive particular spiritual graces that are not the explicit or expected graces.

For example, many young men enter the Jesuit novitiate convinced that God is calling them to be Jesuit priests or brothers. As the two-year novitiate discernment proceeds, they will receive many wonderful graces: a rich prayer life, an ability to live in community, an ability to discern the spirits within, a flexibility that allows for multiple living situations. Some of these men will have been given these graces in order to serve God and the church through the priesthood or brotherhood. But others will receive disconfirmation and will discern that this is not their lifelong calling— that God had called them to the novitiate so that they could receive one or another of these graces and be better prepared to enter their true lifelong calling, such as marriage and family life. God did indeed call them to enter the Jesuits, but not for the reasons that seemed obvious to them.

Consider another example. Right out of college, I've fallen into a job I do really well, and I'm convinced that God is leading me toward a career in this field. Everything seems to point that way—until the company moves to another city and many of my friends and contacts in the industry relocate. I hope to relocate as well, but it seems that one thing after another prevents that from happening. What was God up to, in leading me to several productive years at this workplace? Only years later, when I have found my true lifelong calling do I realize how many business skills I developed while working at that first job. Those skills enable me to do difficult and complex work, now in my lifelong vocation. I never would have learned these skills had I gone straight from college to the vocation to which God was ultimately calling me.

Let's consider a final example. Remember the story of Ray, in chapter 6, whose youngest son wanted so badly to go to the Jesuit school? Ray went through a long discernment process in regard to saying yes to the job transfer. He came to the tentative decision to go with it. He awaited confirmation, but seemed instead to receive disconfirmation. In the end, he decided not take the new job. Was the discernment successful or unsuccessful? If you asked Ray today, he would tell you that God had led him through that discernment in order to remind him of how blessed was his life, just as it was. This unexpected grace was far more important and precious to him than any extra money he would have earned in his new job. The discernment, though it eventually led to disconfirmation and a turning back from a tentative decision, was, in fact, "successful." Ray is a happier, holier man because of it.

Confirmation and the Hesitant or Hasty Decision Maker

If you have identified yourself as a hesitant decision maker, then you need to be careful to guard against the temptation of perpetually seeking confirmation. I do not believe that God typically desires for a person to remain in this awkward in-between place for very long. If you are hesitant, you may need the help of your support network to push you toward a final decision. If, however, you are naturally hasty, this awkward in-between time will seem excruciating! You will want badly to move into the final decision and throw caution to the wind. Hasty decision makers will need the help of their support network to cool their jets and wait patiently for confirmation.

Brother Andrew's Story

I didn't always believe that I was called to be a religious brother. As a young man, I enjoyed dating and looked forward to marriage. When I was twenty-two years old, I had a wonderful relationship with a woman named Liz, and for a while, I was convinced that God wanted me to marry her. Everything in my life seemed to be pointing toward a happy married life with her, and she felt the same way.

We got engaged and began to plan the wedding. Then, out of the blue, Liz broke off the relationship. I was devastated for a while. And even after the heartbreak eased, I wondered what God was up to by drawing me toward Liz only to take her away. Does this mean that I never should have dated her? Was my decision to get engaged a poor discernment on my part? I struggled with this because I felt strongly that God had led me to Liz in the first place.

As time went on I began to sense a calling to join a religious order, the Brothers of the Sacred Heart. Eventually I did so and found myself very happy as a brother. My superiors asked me to work with troubled inner-city youths. It was difficult work, but I enjoyed it and found that I was pretty good at it. Once, on a retreat, I found myself thanking God for my talent in this ministry. It was a complete surprise to me that I could do this work because, in my own youth, I was an uptight and sheltered suburbanite. When did I become so relaxed under pressure? How did I become the sort of person who could deal with the messiness of the impoverished inner city?

And then all of a sudden, it hit me: Liz! It was Liz who taught me to relax and Liz who pushed me out of my sheltered universe and into community-service work with the poor. I never would have found the courage to try it on my own. In my prayer on that retreat, I found myself flooded with emotion as I marveled at the unexpected graces that I received through my relationship with Liz. All along in my dating relationship with her, I thought that God was preparing me for the grace of marriage and family life. Now I see clearly that God had other plans for me and that graces I never dreamed of were offered to me through this relationship. On this retreat, I could finally put to rest the questions about my breakup with Liz. I could finally thank God for disconfirming my choice to marry to her.

Making the Final Decision
and Acting on It

*GOD has opened my ear, and I was not rebellious, I did not turn back-
ward. . . . I have set my face like flint.*

—ISAIAH 50:5, 7

If I have been blessed with confirmation, then it is time to act! When this
moment finally comes, I should act decisively, with the wind—the breath
of God!—at my back. The Old Testament book of Sirach advises, "Do
nothing without deliberation, but when you have acted, do not regret it"
(Sirach 32:19). It would not be unusual to be tempted to second-guess the
decision. Making bold decisions can be scary, and I may at this moment
be tempted to lose my nerve. It is crucial that I not allow the false spirit to
chip away at the joy of having made a well-discerned choice.

Beware of the false spirit at this time.

One example of this last trick of the false spirit concerns a good friend and
fellow Jesuit I'll call Ken. After years of training and formation, Ken was
now ready to begin full-time ministry as a Jesuit priest and professional.
He had several important job offers, two of which seemed particularly conducive to the ministry he had trained for all these years. Ken felt inclined
toward option A, while his superior, who
would make the final decision, felt inclined
toward option B.

> When we have done our
> best, we should wait the
> result in peace.
> —JOHN LUBBOCK

Being trained in the Jesuit method of
discerning, both Ken and his superior spent
many weeks in prayer, discussion, and deliberation. Ultimately, the superior made the final decision to send Ken to option A, the placement Ken
himself desired. Being a part of Ken's support network, I was privileged

to hear the inner movements of Ken's heart as he and the provincial progressed toward the ultimate decision.

Weeks after the decision was made, I told Ken how happy I was that God had blessed him with such a great calling. Ken's face twisted a little as he confessed to me that he was now suffering from guilt and confusion (note the trademarks of the false spirit!). He wondered aloud if perhaps he had manipulated the process to ensure that he would get his way. As I listened to him, I felt the strong presence of desolation in his voice, depriving Ken of the joy of his new assignment. I firmly told Ken that I thought that God had led Ken and his superior to this great choice and that this desolation was the false spirit's desperate attempt to steal back whatever lost ground it could grab. If the spirit of desolation does not succeed in thwarting God's will, then it will try to take a little of the accompanying joy that follows closely behind a decision well made. Ken agreed with this assessment and dismissed the voice of discouragement within him.

He remains in this work today and knows for certain now that the hand of God was in it from the start.

> Was I vacillating when I wanted to do this? Do I make my plans according to ordinary human standards, ready to say "Yes, yes" and "No, no" at the same time? As surely as God is faithful, our word to you has not been "Yes and No." For the Son of God, Jesus Christ . . . was not "Yes and No"; but in him it is always "Yes."
> —2 Corinthians 1:17–19

Strengthen your decision with a pledge.

If the decision is one of lasting import, then after a while, consider making a pledge or firm commitment to the choice you have made—provided there isn't already a vow built in, such as in the case of marriage or religious profession. This, too, is to prevent the false spirit any wiggle room to take back ground you have gained. A religious pledge, commitment, or vow will keep you strong and stable on the days when you feel weak and tempted to turn back.

Making a firm commitment is one way to prepare for desolation while in consolation. If you keep this pledge and are faithful to your commitment for years to come, this in and of itself will bring joy and peace. A well-discerned and sincerely professed pledge or vow will bring consolation because it imitates the steadfastness of God's love for us. "The chooser's happiness," says Dag Hammarskjöld, "lies in his congruence with the chosen." Later on, you may find that the move was not all that you had dreamt it to be. Your pledge or vow is a way of embracing life as it really is rather than as your idealism wanted it to be. It is a way of joining Jesus—as he joins us—in the messiness of human life.

> To bind oneself more to God our Lord and . . . to consecrate oneself completely . . . is a great help toward receiving more abundant grace.
> —St. Ignatius, *Constitutions*, #283

A couple of important points about my firm commitment to this decision:

- It doesn't necessarily have to be a lifelong pledge. If I've decided to break out on my own in my law career, for example, I could promise to give it everything I've got for three years before even considering turning back.
- It is OK for this pledge to be a private one, but I shouldn't keep it a secret from my closest mentors and companions. I must remember that the spirit of desolation loves secrets. The true spirit works in the light.

In the *Spiritual Exercises*, Ignatius warns us not to make a hasty vow. Therefore, before making a final decision, I should thoroughly test my "offering" to make sure that it is indeed the will of God. But once I have done all that I can to confirm this choice with God, I should act with boldness and decisiveness and trust that God will use my actions for my own good and the good of all.

9

Five Things to Remember

For surely I know the plans I have for you, says the LORD, plans for your welfare and not for harm, to give you a future with hope.

—JEREMIAH 29:11

I close with a few thoughts about the process as a whole and about living out the decisions we make.

1. The degree of thoroughness within a discernment process depends upon the gravity of the decision and upon the time allotted to make the decision.

For example, if I am trying to decide whether to bring up a significant, though minor, concern to my boss, the whole process from indifference through the four phases to the final decision might take only a few hours or even a few minutes. But if I am trying to decide whether to get married, or become a priest, or change careers, or move to another city, the discernment process could last for years. In the case of bigger decisions, the timing of the decision itself might need to be discerned. The decision to move from the "gather data" to the "dream the dreams" phase, for example, might be a crucial discernment in and of itself.

2. As I set out to live my commitment, it would be completely natural for me to have buyer's remorse.

As in the story of Ken (see page 205), it would not be unusual for me to second-guess my choice and to doubt one or another step along the way. When I am in a postcommitment desolation, a temptation for me will be to compare the worst days of my current life, living with this commitment, with the best days of my life before I made my commitment. For example, it is not unusual for a novice or seminarian in desolation to start daydreaming about the best days that he had with his girlfriend before entering his current life. He will compare his best days with her with his worst days in the novitiate. The desolation will cause him to forget the reasons he broke up with her in the first place.

3. Waiting for confirmation does not mean waiting until I have certainty before I act.

God never promises certainty. Sometimes I'll have it, but often I won't. Often I'll simply have to make my choice, not knowing for sure that it is the better choice but trusting that God knows my heart and will bless me for the attempt to do his will, even if I accidently miss the mark. This prayer from mystic Thomas Merton has been a source of consolation for many who struggle with having no certainty:

> My Lord God, I have no idea where I am going. I do not see the road ahead of me. I cannot know for certain where it will end. Nor do I really know myself, and the fact that I think that I am following your will does not mean that I am actually doing so.
>
> But I believe that the desire to please you does in fact please you. And I hope I have that desire in all that I am doing. I hope that I will never do anything apart from that desire. And I know that if I do this, you will lead me by the right road though I may know nothing about it.

Therefore will I trust you always though I may seem to be lost
and in the shadow of death. I will not fear; for you are ever with me,
and you will never leave me to face my perils alone.

—THOMAS MERTON, A BOOK OF HOURS, 118*

4. I must have faith that God really will make good come from any sincere choice of mine.

Many believe that in every decision, there is a right choice and several wrong alternatives and that discernment is about figuring out which choice is *the* correct one. In cases which have moral implications (a little girl "discerning" whether or not to shove her little sister into the mud, for example) that assumption is correct. But in cases without serious moral implications (choosing to attend one university over another, for example), it may well be that there is more than one correct choice and that God is ready to bless my life regardless of my choice. St. Ignatius calls this situation "choosing between goods." In these cases, then, what I am seeking is not the correct choice over a series of incorrect ones but rather the choice that is the Magis (the greater). That is, I am seeking the choice that will better aide me in achieving the purpose for which I am created (my principle and foundation). The fact that there may be more than one correct choice should relieve me on the days when I am intimidated by the decision I'm called to make. For example, many young men, in discerning a vocation to the Jesuits, will become distressed with this sort of thinking: *Either God is calling me to be a Jesuit or God is not. If God is calling me to be a Jesuit and I choose not to enter, then my life will be unfulfilled and miserable until the day I die.*

---

*Thomas Merton, *A Book of Hours* (Notre Dame, Ind.: Sorin Books, 2007), 118

Instead of presuming there is one right choice and several wrong ones, perhaps I should presume that God is sending me several *invitations* to do one thing or another. God, being omniscient, knows which choice will bring me the greatest fulfillment, but he loves me enough to allow me to choose. For example, consider my own choice to join the Jesuits. What if I had chosen to ignore the feelings that hit me on January 29? What if I had chosen instead to continue on the path to diocesan priesthood instead of Jesuit priesthood? Or what if I had chosen to pursue having a spouse and family? Would God then have abandoned me had I turned down his offer and chosen one of these other lives? Of course not. In fact, I think I could have been happy in any of those choices. God is like a small-business owner who would be delighted to turn over the business to her son someday. If the son accepts the offer, the owner will teach him the trade and help him along the way. If the son rejects the offer and chooses some other life, she will be right by his side, doing whatever she can to help him achieve his dreams.

5. What *is* crucial, however, is that at any given moment, I choose that which I believe to be the Magis.

What is crucial is my *motivation* for choosing. And what is crucial is that I offer to God this choice and all the other choices of my life. God has given me all these good gifts: family, education, opportunity, a passionate heart, and so on. My great desire is to use these gifts to bring about God's greater praise, reverence, and service—to give back to God the gifts that God has given me. And so, we end our exploration of discernment in the way Ignatius ended the last meditation of his *Spiritual Exercises*, giving all things back to the One who gave all to us:

Take, Lord, and receive all my liberty,

my memory, my understanding

and my entire will,

all that I have and call my own.

You have given it all to me.

To you, Lord, I return it.

Everything is yours; do with it what you will.

Give me only your love and your grace,

that is enough for me.

SE, 234*

---

* As translated in *Hearts on Fire: Praying with Jesuits*, Michael Harter, ed. (Chicago: Loyola Press, 2004), 153.

Index of Figures, Prayer Exercises, and Stories

Figures

Prayer Exercises

Stories

Glossary of Ignatian Terms

Agere contra: Literally, to "act against," the choice to do the opposite of what I am tempted to do in desolation.

Companion: A friend to whom I can entrust the more personal aspects of my life.

Consolation: The state of being under the influence of the true spirit.

Consolation without previous cause: an extraordinary type of consolation in which God consoles a person in a more direct way through a sort of mystical experience rather than as a consequence of a particular external occurrence or internal "course of thoughts."

Desolation: The state of being under the influence of the false spirit.

Examen: A quick daily reflection on the spirits that have stirred my thoughts, emotions, and actions this day.

False consolation: The experience of being drawn to feelings, thoughts, and actions that look good and holy at first but ultimately lead to actions that the person is not called by God to do at this time.

False spirit: The "inner pull" away from God's plan and away from faith, hope, and love. The false spirit is also referred to as "the evil spirit" or "the enemy of our human nature."

First principle and foundation: The statement that answers the big questions about the purpose of my life and the purpose of this decision.

Hasty decision maker: Someone who tends to jump too quickly into a decision, someone who makes a decision without thoroughly discerning.

Hesitant decision maker: Someone who drags his or her feet in making a decision, usually because the decision requires an uncomfortable choice.

217

Ignatian indifference: The grace-filled state of desiring to do God's will and to praise, reverence, and serve God more than desiring anything else. The state of grateful availability.

Ignatian intuition: The internal ability to perceive the movements of the two spirits within me.

Magis: Dreaming of the greater glory of God. The desire to choose that which gives God more glory.

Prayer life: Through prayer, my ongoing intimate relationship with God.

Spiritual direction: The process of meeting regularly with a person trained to help me with my relationship with God.

Support network: Mentors, companions, and the church

True spirit: The "inner pull" toward God's plan and toward faith, hope, and love. It is also referred to as "the good spirit."

Related Bible Passages

Deuteronomy 30:11–20	I have set before you life and death. Choose life.
1 Samuel 16:1–13	Samuel chooses David over his brothers.
1 Kings 3:1–15	Lord, give me wisdom to judge right from wrong.
Psalm 23	The Lord is my shepherd.
Psalm 107:4–9	The Lord answers our distress call.
Wisdom 9:1–18b	Give me wisdom that sits by your throne.
Sirach 14:20–27	Happy is the one who meditates on wisdom.
Isaiah 30:15–21	By waiting you shall be told, "This is the way, walk in it."
Isaiah 42:1–16	God will lead the blind . . . by paths unknown.
Isaiah 55	God's ways are not our ways.
Jeremiah 29:11–14	"I know well the plans I have for you"
Jeremiah 31:31–34	God will write the law inside us.
Matthew 7:7–8	On prayer and discernment.
Matthew 7:13–14	"Enter through the narrow gate."
Matthew 9:35–38	They were like sheep without a shepherd.
Mark 10:46–52	The blind man Bartimaeus: "I want to see!"
John 10:1–18	They know the Shepherd's voice.
John 14:1–14	Lord, we do not know the way.
Romans 8	On prayer and discernment
2 Corinthians 1:17–20	Jesus is not yes and no, but only yes.
2 Corinthians 4:16–18	We fix our gaze on what is unseen.

2 Corinthians 11:3–15	"My fear is that your thoughts will be corrupted."
Ephesians 5:8–20	Try to discern the will of the Lord.
Philippians 1:9–11	Learn to value the things that really matter.
Philippians 1:12–26	"I don't know which to choose: to live or to die."
Philippians 4:4–9	Dismiss all anxiety.
Colossians 3:1–17	Set your heart on the higher things.
1 John 4	Test the spirits to see whether they are from God.

Suggestions for Further Reading

Timothy Gallagher has written excellent books exploring Ignatius of Loyola's Rules for Discernment of Spirits, among them *The Discernment of Spirits* (Crossroad, 2005) and *Spiritual Consolation* (Crossroad, 2007). Thomas H. Green's *Weeds among the Wheat* (Ave Maria, 2005) is one of my all-time favorite books on discernment. David Lonsdale's *Listening to the Music of the Spirit* (Ave Maria, 1993) is unfortunately out of print but remains very popular.

The primary texts of the writings of St. Ignatius of Loyola as well as more scholarly treatments of those writings can be found at the Institute of Jesuit Sources (www.jesuitsources.com).

I strongly recommend *any* books by the following Jesuit authors: George A. Aschenbrenner, William Barry, Gerald Fagin, David L. Fleming, Richard Hauser, James Martin, Joseph Tetlow.

If you would like to learn more about spiritual direction or to find a spiritual director in your area, www.sdiworld.org is a good place to start.

Some of my favorite sites to visit on the Web are the following

United States Conference of Catholic Bishops
http://www.usccb.org/

Loyola Press
http://www.loyolapress.com/

Jesuits Online
http://www.jesuit.org/

Creighton University's Online Ministries

http://onlineministries.creighton.edu/CollaborativeMinistry/online
.html

American Catholic

http://www.americancatholic.org/

A layman's experience of prayer

http://writingsbysteveblog.com/wordpress/

Primary Text of Ignatius's
Rules for Discernment of Spirits

St. Ignatius's
Rules for Discernment of Spirits,
First Week

Rules for understanding to some extent the different movements produced in the soul and for recognizing those that are good, to admit them, and those that are bad, to reject them. These rules are more suited to the first week.

1. In the case of those who go from one mortal sin to another, the enemy is ordinarily accustomed to propose apparent pleasures. He fills their imagination with sensual delights and gratifications, the more readily to keep them in their vices and increase the number of their sins.

With such persons the good spirit uses a method which is the reverse of the above. Making use of the light of reason, he will rouse the sting of conscience and fill them with remorse.

2. In the case of those who go on earnestly striving to cleanse their souls from sin and who seek to rise in the service of God our Lord to greater perfection, the method pursued is the opposite of that mentioned in the first rule.

Then it is characteristic of the evil spirit to harass with anxiety, to afflict with sadness, to raise obstacles backed by fallacious reasonings that disturb the soul. Thus he seeks to prevent the soul from advancing.

It is characteristic of the good spirit, however, to give courage and strength, consolations, tears, inspirations, and peace. This He does by making all easy, by removing all obstacles so that the soul goes forward in doing good.

3. **Spiritual Consolation.** I call it consolation when an interior movement is aroused in the soul, by which it is inflamed with love of its Creator and Lord, and as a consequence, can love no creature on the face of the earth for its own sake, but only in the Creator of them all. It is likewise consolation when one sheds tears that move to the love of God, whether it be because of sorrow for sins, or because of the sufferings of Christ our Lord, or for any other reason that is immediately directed to the praise and service of God. Finally, I call consolation every increase of faith, hope, and love, and all interior joy that invites and attracts to what is heavenly and to the salvation of one's soul by filling it with peace and quiet in its Creator and Lord.

4. **Spiritual Desolation.** I call desolation what is entirely the opposite of what is described in the third rule, as darkness of soul, turmoil of spirit, inclination to what is low and earthly, restlessness rising from many disturbances and temptations which lead to want of faith, want of hope, want of love. The soul is wholly slothful, tepid, sad, and separated, as it were, from its Creator and Lord. For just as consolation is the opposite of desolation, so the thoughts that spring from consolation are the opposite of those that spring from desolation.

5. In time of desolation we should never make any change, but remain firm and constant in the resolution and decision which guided us the day before the desolation, or in the decision to which we adhered in the preceding consolation. For just as in consolation the good spirit guides and counsels us, so in desolation the evil spirit guides and counsels. Following his counsels we can never find the way to a right decision.

6. Though in desolation we must never change our former resolutions, it will be very advantageous to intensify our activity against the

desolation. We can insist more upon prayer, upon meditation, and on much examination of ourselves. We can make an effort in a suitable way to do some penance.

7. When one is in desolation, he should be mindful that God has left him to his natural powers to resist the different agitations and temptations of the enemy in order to try him. He can resist with the help of God, which always remains, though he may not clearly perceive it. For though God has taken from him the abundance of fervor and overflowing love and the intensity of His favors, nevertheless, he has sufficient grace for eternal salvation.

8. When one is in desolation, he should strive to persevere in patience. This reacts against the vexations that have overtaken him. Let him consider, too, that consolation will soon return, and in the meantime, he must diligently use the means against desolation which have been given in the sixth rule.

9. The principal reasons why we suffer from desolation are three:

The first is because we have been tepid and slothful or negligent in our exercises of piety, and so through our own fault spiritual consolation has been taken away from us.

The second reason is because God wishes to try us, to see how much we are worth, and how much we will advance in His service and praise when left without the generous reward of consolations and signal favors.

The third reason is because God wishes to give us a true knowledge and understanding of ourselves, so that we may have an intimate perception of the fact that it is not within our power to acquire and attain great devotion, intense love, tears, or any other spiritual consolation; but that all this is the gift and grace of God our Lord. God does not wish us to build on the property of another, to rise up in spirit in a certain pride and vainglory and attribute to ourselves the devotion and other effects of spiritual consolation.

10. When one enjoys consolation, let him consider how he will conduct himself during the time of ensuing desolation, and store up a supply of strength as defense against that day.

11. He who enjoys consolation should take care to humble himself and lower himself as much as possible. Let him recall how little he is able to do in time of desolation, when he is left without such grace or consolation.

On the other hand, one who suffers desolation should remember that by making use of the sufficient grace offered him, he can do much to withstand all his enemies. Let him find his strength in his Creator and Lord.

12. The enemy conducts himself as a woman. He is a weakling before a show of strength, and a tyrant if he has his will. It is characteristic of a woman in a quarrel with a man to lose courage and take to flight if the man shows that he is determined and fearless. However, if the man loses courage and begins to flee, the anger, vindictiveness, and rage of the woman surge up and know no bounds. In the same way, the enemy becomes weak, loses courage, and turns to flight with his seductions as soon as one leading a spiritual life faces his temptations boldly, and does exactly the opposite of what he suggests. However, if one begins to be afraid and to lose courage in temptations, no wild animal on earth can be more fierce than the enemy of our human nature. He will carry out his perverse intentions with consummate malice.

13. Our enemy may also be compared in his manner of acting to a false lover. He seeks to remain hidden and does not want to be discovered. If such a lover speaks with evil intention to the daughter of a good father, or to the wife of a good husband, and seeks to seduce them, he wants his words and solicitations kept secret. He is greatly displeased if his evil suggestions and depraved intentions are revealed by the daughter to her father, or by the wife to her husband. Then he readily sees he will not succeed in what he has begun. In the same way, when the enemy of our human nature tempts a just soul with his wiles and seductions, he earnestly desires that

they be received secretly and kept secret. But if one manifests them to a confessor, or to some other spiritual person who understands his deceits and malicious designs, the evil one is very much vexed. For he knows that he cannot succeed in his evil undertaking, once his evident deceits have been revealed.

14. The conduct of our enemy may also be compared to the tactics of a leader intent upon seizing and plundering a position he desires. A commander and leader of an army will encamp, explore the fortifications and defenses of the stronghold, and attack at the weakest point. In the same way, the enemy of our human nature investigates from every side all our virtues, theological, cardinal, and moral. Where he finds the defenses of eternal salvation weakest and most deficient, there he attacks and tries to take us by storm.

Rules for Discernment of Spirits, Second Week

Further rules for understanding the different movements produced in the soul. They serve for a more accurate discernment of spirits and are more suitable for the second week.

1. It is characteristic of God and His Angels, when they act upon the soul, to give true happiness and spiritual joy, and to banish all the sadness and disturbances which are caused by the enemy.

It is characteristic of the evil one to fight against such happiness and consolation by proposing fallacious reasonings, subtleties, and continual deceptions.

2. God alone can give consolation to the soul without any previous cause. It belongs solely to the Creator to come into a soul, to leave it, to act upon it, to draw it wholly to the love of His Divine Majesty. I said without previous cause, that is, without any preceding perception or knowledge of any subject by which a soul might be led to such a consolation through its own acts of intellect and will.

3. If a cause precedes, both the good angel and the evil spirit can give consolation to a soul, but for a quite different purpose. The good angel consoles for the progress of the soul, that it may advance and rise to what is more perfect. The evil spirit consoles for purposes that are the contrary, and that afterwards he might draw the soul to his own perverse intentions and wickedness.

4. It is a mark of the evil spirit to assume the appearance of an angel of light. He begins by suggesting thoughts that are suited to a devout soul, and ends by suggesting his own. For example, he will suggest holy and pious thoughts that are wholly in conformity with the sanctity of the soul. Afterwards, he will endeavor little by little to end by drawing the soul into his hidden snares and evil designs.

5. We must carefully observe the whole course of our thoughts. If the beginning and middle and end of the course of thoughts are wholly good and directed to what is entirely right, it is a sign that they are from the good angel. But the course of thoughts suggested to us may terminate in something evil, or distracting, or less good than the soul had formerly proposed to do. Again, it may end in what weakens the soul, or disquiets it; or by destroying the peace, tranquility, and quiet which it had before, it may cause disturbance to the soul. These things are a clear sign that the thoughts are proceeding from the evil spirit, the enemy of our progress and eternal salvation.

6. When the enemy of our human nature has been detected and recognized by the trail of evil marking his course and by the wicked end to which he leads us, it will be profitable for one who has been tempted to review immediately the whole course of the temptation. Let him consider the series of good thoughts, how they arose, how the evil one gradually attempted to make him step down from the state of spiritual delight and joy in which he was, till finally he drew him to his wicked designs. The purpose of this review is that once such an experience has been understood and carefully observed, we may guard ourselves for the future against the customary deceits of the enemy.

7. In souls that are progressing to greater perfection, the action of the good angel is delicate, gentle, delightful. It may be compared to a drop of water penetrating a sponge.

The action of the evil spirit upon such souls is violent, noisy, and disturbing. It may be compared to a drop of water falling upon a stone.

In souls that are going from bad to worse, the action of the spirits mentioned above is just the reverse. The reason for this is to be sought in the opposition or similarity of these souls to the different kinds of spirits. When the disposition is contrary to that of the spirits, they enter with noise and commotion that are easily perceived. When the disposition is similar to that of the spirits, they enter silently, as one coming into his own house when the doors are open.

8. When consolation is without previous cause, as was said, there can be no deception in it, since it can proceed from God our Lord only. But a spiritual person who has received such a consolation must consider it very attentively, and must cautiously distinguish the actual time of the consolation from the period which follows it. At such a time the soul is still fervent and favored with the grace and aftereffects of the consolation which has passed. In this second period the soul frequently forms various resolutions and plans which are not granted directly by God our Lord. They may come from our own reasoning on the relations of our concepts and on the consequences of our judgments, or they may come from the good or evil spirit. Hence, they must be carefully examined before they are given full approval and put into execution.

SOURCE: LOUIS J. PUHL, *THE SPIRITUAL EXERCISES OF ST. IGNATIUS: BASED ON STUDIES IN THE LANGUAGE OF THE AUTOGRAPH*, (CHICAGO: LOYOLA PRESS, 1968).